Robert Herrick, Ernest Rhys

The Lyric Poems of Robert Herrick

Robert Herrick, Ernest Rhys

The Lyric Poems of Robert Herrick

ISBN/EAN: 9783744779487

Printed in Europe, USA, Canada, Australia, Japan

Cover: Foto ©Thomas Meinert / pixelio.de

More available books at **www.hansebooks.com**

THE LYRIC POEMS OF ROBERT HERRICK.

·EDITED·BY·ERNEST·
RHYS·

J·M·DENT·&Co· ALDINE·HOUSE·
60 Qt EASTERN·St LONDON·E.C·

CONTENTS

v

Contents.

Contents.

Contents.

Contents.

Contents.

Contents.

Contents.

INTRODUCTION.

Herrick follows Campion closely in the natural order of the lyric poets, but though the two poets have many points of contact, he owes nothing directly to his exquisite forerunner. He did, on the other hand, owe a very great deal to Ben Jonson, and is to be counted, for all critical ends and purposes, among the redoubtable "Sons of Ben." His five poems addressed to his master, especially his brief ode and the "lyric feasts" of which it speaks,—

> " Made at the Sun,
> The Dog, the Triple Tun,"

recall at once the famous Fleet - Street Academe, in which he studied to some purpose. If, in that school for poets, Jonson's "Underwoods" may count as the academic groves, then Herrick's "Hesperides" were the late last fruits from their noble stock.

From his father in poetry, Herrick learnt admirable doctrine. He learnt to qualify the Elizabethan music with a Latin note, without losing anything of the finer impulse of his own tongue. He kept his lyric simplicity, and never let the new influences, which waxed hot in Donne and grew cold in

Introduction.

Cowley, so much as breathe upon his verse.
Ben Jonson, and his own genius and born
sense of the lyric style, defended him against
the fleeting fashions of the pseudo-meta-
physical poetry. Indeed, his poems, which
casual readers have thought artless, are really
the result of consummate art, and of the
happiest combination of natural inspiration
and conscious craftsmanship. In earlier youth,
he was for a time a goldsmith's apprentice,
and it is not too fanciful, perhaps, to con-
sider, as some critics have done, that he
gained something of his sense of form, and
his fine art of turning the lyric into a sort
of tiny and finished jewel, from his experi-
ences in his uncle's workshop in Golden
Cheapside.

In Golden Cheapside ("Golden," partly
because of the goldsmiths' shops that abounded
there, partly because of the cross at the end of
Wood-Street and other such gilded splendours;)
he was born, in August 1591. On the 24th of
that month he was baptised at St Vedast's
Church, Foster Lane, where his father,
Nicholas Herrick, also practised the goldsmith's craft. Nicholas died, under suspicion
of suicide, by a fall from an upper window
of his house, in 1592. The suspicion is borne
out by the action of the Bishop of Bristol,
who, as High Almoner, attempted to sequester
the goods and chattels of the deceased on
grounds of "*felo-de-se*"; and succeeded in
compounding his claim for £220. Meanwhile
the dead goldsmith's family, eight in number,

Introduction.

left town for Hampton Court, where a pos-
thumous child was born, "at Harry Campion's
house," a name which, under the circum-
stances, sounds suggestive. Robert, who more
than once recalls Hampton with delight in his
poems, was the youngest but one in the family.
His school-days, according to the little evidence
we have, were probably passed between Hampton and London. When he left school, in
1607, he was apprenticed for ten years to his
uncle William, a younger brother of Nicholas
Herrick, who still carried on his business, in
which, it is likely, the widow still retained an
interest. With his uncle, the poet did not,
evidently, find himself much in sympathy;
and a lyric fancy is not the best reconciler,
when one is young, and one's elders and
every-day avocation grow tedious.

Before his apprenticeship had run out,
Herrick succeeded in persuading his uncle
that the goldsmith's was not his destined
rôle, and he was entered as an undergraduate of St John's College, Cambridge.
It is quite possible that he effected this step
by diplomatically hinting a decided leaning to
the law; for with his guardian, who was on
the way to make a fortune after gaining a
knighthood, the law was like to be an in-
telligible argument; while he himself, no
doubt, saw in the law only a convenient
ladder to other things, with poetry at the
top of all. At Cambridge, his uncle kept
him on a rather straitened allowance, as
we find from more than one appeal, written

Introduction.

in amusingly euphuistic terms, as if to make
an impression on a guardian who was to
be affected by a certain parade of Latin
and fine phrases. On grounds of economy,
the undergraduate presently converted himself from a law to an arts student, and
migrated from St John's to Trinity Hall,
on the time-honoured plea of the Church.
This only shews again that he had no very
clear idea of what he wanted to do, beyond
putting himself in the liberal way to be a
poet and a gentleman, and to get as much
entertainment out of life as possible. But
how did he live on leaving Cambridge? He
did not take his M.A. till 1620. He did not
receive his presentation to the vicarage of
Dean Prior until nine years later. Probably
he contrived to exist on the residue of
the small means—some four or five hundred
pounds—which came to him from his father's
estate; and to study life and cultivate the lyric
arts in London in his own way, sitting at the
feet of Ben Jonson. It is clear that he entered
with zest into the life which some of his
poems, actively or retrospectively inspired,
written then or afterwards, suggest:

" Wild I am now with heat;
  O Bacchus, cool thy rays!
  Or frantic, I shall eat
  The thyrse, and bite the bays.

" Round, round, the roof does run;
  And being ravished thus,
  Come, I will drink a tun
  To my Propertius!"

Introduction.

This is no divinity student's note. In his "Farewell unto Poetrie" he is still more explicit. They kept it up in those days, as he reminds us in his most extravagant lines : morning, noon, and night ; nay, "past noon of night," and so on again, through "the fresh and fairest flourish of the morn" ; fleeting the time,

" With flame and rapture, drinking to the odd
Number of wine, which makes us full with God.
And in that mystic frenzy, we have hurled
(As with a tempest) nature through the world,
And in a whirl-wind twirl'd her home, aghast
At that which in her ecstasy had past."

Fortunately, if Ben Jonson lent his sanction to this valiant roystering, he did not let the illusions of sack disguise the true severity of poetry. He laid down the law for his sons with no uncertain sound. No son of mine, he said in effect, and how plainly one seems to hear him say it !—will think "he can leap forth suddenly a poet by dreaming he hath been in Parnassus, or by having washt his lips, as they say, in Helicon. There goes more to his making than so ; for to Nature, Exercise, Imitation, and Study, Art must be added, to make all these perfect. And though these challenge much to themselves in the making up of our maker, it is Art only can lead him to perfection." This is very good gospel, and in Herrick's case it fell on plastic ears.

" Let's strive to be the best ! the Gods, we know it,
Pillars and men, hate an indifferent poet."

Introduction.

There is the same text paraphrased from Horace by himself; excellently concentrated in a couplet. To these splendid follies and Jonsonian dissertations over liberal sack and the rarer vintage of the "Underwoods" and the "Forest," Herrick, all too soon for his own satisfaction, was to bid good-bye. His four or five hundred pounds could not last long, under stress of the lyric levees at "The Sun, the Dog, the Triple Tun." In 1829, as we said, he was presented to Dean Prior, and Devonshire seemed the end of the world to him.

His "Farewell unto Poetrie," already quoted from, was written no doubt at this time; evidently he thought he was bidding farewell not only to town but to poetry. As a matter of fact, his own poetry was only at its beginning. Almost all the poems which have done most to win him a familiar fame in our own time—such lyrics as "To Daffadils," "To Blossoms," and the rest—were written after he went

> ". . . to banishment
> Into the loathèd West."

It was there, in the "dull Devonshire," that bored him often to extinction, that he found the lyric moments which inspired those golden rhymes of the country life, its festivals and its flowers, by which he chiefly has his fame in the wider world that is not literary. He carried his Catullus to the country with him, and the Devonshire daffodils and "July flowers," the village maids and rural feasts,

Introduction.

did the rest. If he had remained in London, he might have been lost in the indistinctive crowd of the minor poets, so far as the world's recognition of him went. Even as it was, it was to take a couple of centuries to gild his laurel.

Of Dean Bourne itself, I cannot do better than quote from Mr Grosart's pleasant account of the place. From Brent, which lies some sixteen miles from Plymouth, the road approaches by quiet hamlets and pleasant meadows, with here and there glimpses of distant hills ; and presently, fording a stream, where a little stone foot-bridge crosses alongside, reaches the narrow lane which leads down to Dean Church. Here, looking down from the high-road, the traveller sees the church and vicarage, with surrounding farm-buildings and cottages, set amid trees in a deep and narrow valley. Dean Prior lies about a mile further on. The "rude River. . . by which sometime he lived,"—Dean Bourne, flows down through the court and passes close to Dean Prior.

There, in that lonely vicarage, with his maid and housekeeper, Prue ; his spaniel, Tracy ; his pet lamb or pet pig ; his hens and his geese ; and, if we take the plain testimony of his "Thanksgiving," his cows he settled down into the pastoral life which suited his genius better than it did his London-bred tastes. Both his disgust and his delight are vigorously expressed by him at different moments, according to his mood.

Introduction.

His memories of Golden Cheapside, and of
Fleet - Street, and the tavern nights of old,
continually haunt him.

> " London my home is ; though by hard fate sent
> Into a long and irksome banishment ;
> Yet since call'd back, henceforward let me be,
> O native country, repossess'd by thee ! "

This he wrote in 1648, when with his fellow
parsons, he was ejected on the coming of the
Commonwealth. He was then fifty-seven,
and he returned to town, only to find it sadly
changed. It seems the thought of London,
and the necessity of reminding his friends there
of his existence, and his present predicament,
prompted him at last to collect his poems,
previously only published, to the number of
some sixty pieces, in "Wit's Recreations."
In 1648 his book, " Hesperides," and " Noble
Numbers," was published—not with any con-
spicuous success. His old circle, indeed, was
by this time broken up. Ben Jonson was
gone, and his influence had waned. So the
" Hesperides," anything but "timely fortunate," as their poet wished, must be
counted among the books that have missed,
in their author's lifetime, their golden
moment.
    Three years before Herrick's return to
London, Milton's earlier poems had appeared ;
but it was not Milton, but Cowley, who
marks for us the taste and fashion in poetry
of the time. Cowley's poems, excellently
second-rate ; finely conceived, admirably

Introduction.

phrased, but hardly inspired ; ran through
edition after edition in this period. Herrick's passed all but unnoticed. The same
thing goes on in every period ; and no
doubt we have our over-indulged Cowleys
and our overlooked Herricks to-day. There
is the consolation of those who do not please
their public, and wish to believe they write
poems for posterity.

With the publication of the " Hesperides "
and the " Noble Numbers," Herrick's career
as a poet closes. The years intervening, ere
the Restoration restored him, too, to his living
at Dean Prior, were not, clearly, fortunate
ones for him. His income, in spite of the
stated provision for outlawed parsonry, soon
dwindled to almost nothing. He had rich
relations, it is true ; but what is the pro-
verbial lot of the poor relation? And
Herrick had a restless wit, quite apt to
revenge itself for meagre hospitalities and to
alarm diffident hosts. In the end he was as
glad to get back to his parishioners, and to
his dull Devonshire, as he had previously been
to leave them. He died at Dean Prior in
1674, at the ripe age of eighty-four, and was
buried in the church, where now a memorial
tablet commemorates him.

Of his fame, if he sometimes expressed a
naïve mistrust of it, he felt fairly secure, it
is clear, on the whole. Mr Andrew Lang
once objected, in a lost leader, to the rhyming
of " Herrick " with " lyric " by a modern
rhymer, but Herrick himself was fond of the

Introduction.

rhyme, used it more than once, and in the following quatrain used it yet again, to emphasise his faith in himself and his poetry :

> " Thou shalt not all die ; for while Love's fire shines
> Upon his altar, men shall read thy lines ;
> And learn'd musicians shall, to honour Herrick's
> Fame, and his name, both set and sing his lyrics."

Herrick quite accepted the theory that lyric poetry must hold to music as well as to prosody. He was not, like Campion, a musician himself, but he shews in numerous places in the " Hesperides" how much music counted to him. To Henry Lawes, in particular, who set some six poems of his, Herrick wrote eight lines, in which he mentions also Jacques Gouter, and other famous lutinists and musicians of the time :

> Touch but thy lyre, my Harry, and I hear
> From thee some raptures of the rare Gotiere :
> Then if thy voice commingle with the string,
> I hear in thee the rare Laniere to sing,
> Or curious Wilson. Tell me, canst thou be
> Less than Apollo, that usurp'st such three,
> Three unto whom the whole world gave applause ?
> Yet their three praises praise but one :
> > That's Lawes."

In his valuable notes to the little volume of Herrick, in the Canterbury Series, Mr H. P. Horne reminds us that Lawes set to music poems by Milton, Lovelace, Carew, and Ben Jonson, and adds, "at the present day he is

Introduction.

chiefly remembered for having composed, in 1634, the songs for 'Comus.' He published several books of music, and amongst them his 'Choice Psalms' in 1648, for which Milton wrote the sonnet addressed to him." Lawes, it is interesting to note, learnt music from that Coperio, or Coprario (John Cooper, to wit), who was associated with Campion. Beside those set by Lawes, it is evident that many other of Herrick's poems were specially written, and are perfectly devised, for music, as various settings, old and new, may shew.

A natural ear for music, in both kinds; a lyrical fancy; a consummate sense of words; a fortunate schooling at the hands of Ben Jonson and certain Elizabethans, or of Catullus, Horace, and Martial; a congenial life for poetry, although in a London that was perhaps too lively, and a Devonshire that was too dull; all these were Herrick's, and went to make him what he was. Like Campion, he had an ear for music, but he never sacrificed a single song to the exigencies of a lute or theorbo. Like Donne, he had a subtle wit, but he rarely sacrificed a poem for the sake of even a finest conceit. And if his pastoral tunes have a classic accompaniment, and his love-lyrical note recalls other Julias than those of a Jacobean London, everything he wrote, good and bad, is unmistakeably "toucht (like lawful plate)," as he claims; unmistakeably and inimitably his own.

In all English lyric poetry, there are very few to compare with him. You may begin with

Introduction.

Tennyson, and count only a score of names backwards, and then reduce the score to a scant half dozen, and still Herrick's note is heard, clear, distinct above all. Indeed, that note, so long neglected, is now grown almost too familiar, so that we are in danger, perhaps, of forgetting how fine it is. This as it may be, Herrick, as much as Burns or Shelley, can count to-day on that greater public, who know not Campion, and to whom his rare master, Ben Jonson, is little more than a name.

E. R.

—◦◦◦—

The Argument
of his Book.

Hesperides. " Hock-carts " (l. 3) were the last carts in from the harvest-field. " Wakes" were not funeral, but village feasts.

I SING of brooks, of blossomes, birds, and
  bowers :
Of April, May, of June, and July-flowers.
I sing of May-poles, hock-carts, wassails,
  wakes,
Of bride-grooms, brides, and of their bridall-
  cakes.
I write of youth, of love, and have accesse
By these, to sing of cleanly-wantonnesse.
I sing of dewes, of raines, and piece by piece
Of balme, of oyle, of spice, and amber-greece.
I sing of times trans-shifting ; and I write
How roses first came red, and lillies white.
I write of groves, of twilights, and I sing
The court of Mab, and of the Fairie-king.
I write of hell ; I sing, and ever shall,
Of heaven, and hope to have it after all.

Lyric Poems.

To his Muse.

Hesperides. "Coats"
(l. 5), cotes, cots. "Neat"
(l. 13), Oxen.

Wₕₗₜₕₑᵣ, mad maiden, wilt thou roame?
Farre safer 'twere to stay at home;
Where thou mayst sit, and piping please
The poore and private cottages.
Since coats and hamlets best agree
With this thy meaner minstralsie.
There with the reed, thou mayest expresse
The shepherds fleecy happinesse:
And with thy eclogues intermixe
Some smooth and harmlesse beucolicks.
There on a hillock thou mayst sing
Unto a handsome shephardling;
Or to a girle (that keeps the neat)
With breath more sweet then violet.
There, there, perhaps, such lines as these
May take the simple villages.
But for the court, the country wit
Is despicable unto it.
Stay then at home, and doe not goe
Or flie abroad to seeke for woe.
Contempts in courts and cities dwell;
No critick haunts the poore mans cell:
Where thou mayst hear thine own lines read
By no one tongue, there, censured.
That man's unwise will search for ill,
And may prevent it, sitting still.

—ᴧᴧᴧ—

2

Herrick.

To his Booke. Hesperides.

I.

WHILE thou didst keep thy candor undefil'd,
Deerely I lov'd thee, as my first-borne child :
But when I saw thee wantonly to roame
From house to house, and never stay at home ;
I brake my bonds of love, and bad thee goe,
Regardlesse whether well thou sped'st, or no.
On'with thy fortunes then, what e'er they be ;
If good I'le smile, if bad I'le sigh for thee.

II.

To read my booke the virgin shie
May blush, while Brutus standeth by :
But when he's gone, read through what's writ,
And never staine a cheeke for it.

—ᴡᴧᴧᴧ—

When He would have his Verses Read.

Hesperides. "Thyrse"
(l. 7), "A javelin twind
with ivy." Orgies (l. 8),
"Songs to Bacchus."—
(HERRICK).

IN sober mornings, doe not thou reherse
The holy incantation of a verse ;
But when that men have both well drunke, and
    fed,
Let my enchantments then be sung, or read.

3

Lyric Poems.

When laurell spirts i'th' fire, and when the
    hearth
Smiles to it selfe, and guilds the roofe with
    mirth ;
When up the thryse is rais'd, and when the
    sound
Of sacred orgies flyes, A round, a round.
When the rose raignes, and locks with oint-
    ments shine,
Let rigid Cato read these lines of mine.

—∿∿∿—

To live Merrily, and to trust to Good Verses.

Hesperides. " Pap " (l.
7), sap. " Retorted " (l.
12), tossed back.

Now is the time for mirth,
    Nor cheek, or tongue be dumbe :
For with the flowrie earth,
    The golden pomp is come.

The golden pomp is come ;
    For now each tree do's weare,
Made of her pap and gum,
    Rich beads of amber here.

Now raignes the rose, and now
    Th' Arabian dew besmears
My uncontrolled brow,
    And my retorted haires.

4

Herrick.

Homer, this health to thee,
  In sack of such a kind,
That it wo'd make thee see,
  Though thou wert ne'er so blind.

Next, Virgil, Ile call forth,
  To pledge this second health
In wine, whose each cup's worth
  An Indian common-wealth.

A goblet next Ile drink
  To Ovid ; and suppose,
Made he the pledge, he'd think
  The world had all one nose.

Then this immensive cup
  Of aromatike wine,
Catullus, I quaffe up
  To that terce muse of thine.

Wild I am now with heat ;
  O Bacchus ! coole thy raies !
Or frantick I shall eate
  Thy thyrse, and bite the bayes.

Round, round, the roof do's run ;
  And being ravisht thus,
Come, I will drink a tun
  To my Propertius.

Now, to Tibullus, next,
  This flood I drink to thee :
But stay ; I see a text,
  That this presents to me.

Lyric Poems.

Behold, Tibullus lies
   Here burnt, whose smal return
Of ashes, scarce suffice
   To fill a little urne.

Trust to good verses then ;
   They onely will aspire,
When pyramids, as men,
   Are lost, i'th'funerall fire.

And when all bodies meet
   In Lethe to be drown'd ;
Then onely Numbers sweet,
   With endless life are crown'd.

—⁓⋏⋀⋀⋎⋏⋎—

The Parliament of Roses.

To Julia.—Hesperides.

I DREAMT the roses one time went
To meet and sit in parliament :
The place for these, and for the rest
Of flowers, was thy spotlesse breast :
Over the which a state was drawne
Of Tiffanie, or cob-web lawne ;
Then in that parly, all those powers
Voted the rose, the Queen of flowers.
But so, as that herself should be
The maide of honour unto thee.

6

Herrick.

The Rosarie. esperides.

ONE ask'd me where the roses grew?
I bade him not goe seek ;
But forthwith bade my Julia shew
A bud in either cheek.

—ᴧᴧᴧᴧ—

Cherrie-ripe. Hesperides.

CHERRIE-ripe, ripe, ripe, I cry,
Full and faire ones ; come, and buy :
If so be, you ask me where
They doe grow? I answer, There,
Where my Julia's lips doe smile ;
There's the land, or Cherry-ile :
Whose plantations fully show
All the yeere, where cherries grow.

—ᴧᴧᴧᴧ—

Upon Julia's Voice. Hesperides.

So smooth, so sweet, so silv'ry is thy voice,
As, could they hear, the damn'd would make
    no noise ;
But listen to thee, walking in thy chamber,
Melting melodious words to lutes of amber.

7

Lyric Poems.

Againe.

WHEN I thy singing next shall heare,
Ile wish I might turne all to eare,
To drink in notes, and numbers, such
As blessed soules cann't heare too much :
Then melted down, there let me lye
Entranc'd, and lost confusedly :
And by thy musique strucken mute,
Die, and be turn'd into a lute.

—◁◁◁—

Upon Roses. Hesperides.

UNDER a lawne, then skyes more cleare,
Some ruffled roses nestling were ;
And snugging there, they seem'd to lye
As in a flowrie nunnery :
They blush'd, and look'd more fresh than
    flowers
Quickned of late by pearly showers ;
And all, because they were possest
But of the heat of Julia's breast :
Which as a warme, and moistned spring,
Gave them their ever flourishing.

—◁◁◁—

8

Herrick.

To Julia.

"Dardanium" (l. 8).
"A bracelet, from Dardanus so call'd."—
HERRICK. Hesperides.

How rich and pleasing thou, my Julia, art,
In each thy dainty, and peculiar part !
First, for thy queen-ship on thy head is set
Of flowers a sweet commingled coronet :
About thy neck a carkanet is bound,
Made of the rubie, pearle, and diamond :
A golden ring, that shines upon thy thumb :
About thy wrist, the rich Dardanium.
Between thy breast, then doune of swans more
        white,
There playes the saphire with the chrysolite.
No part besides must of thy selfe be known,
But by the topaz, opal, calcedon.

—◊◊◊—

The Rock of Rubies.

"And the Quarrie of Pearls." Hesperides.

Some ask'd me where the rubies grew ?
    And nothing I did say ;
But with my finger pointed to
    The lips of Julia.
Some ask'd how pearls did grow, and where ?
    Then spoke I to my girle,
To part her lips, and shew'd them there
    The quarelets of pearl.

9

Upon Julia's Haire fill'd with Dew.

Hesperides.

DEW sate on Julia's haire,
    And spangled too,
Like leaves that laden are
    With trembling dew :
Or glitter'd to my sight,
    As when the beames
Have their reflected light,
    Daunc't by the streames.

—✧—

Upon Julia's Recovery.

Hesperides.

DROOP, droop no more, or hang the head,
Ye roses almost withered ;
Now strength, and newer purple get,
Each here declining violet.
O primroses ! let this day be
A resurrection unto ye ;
And to all flowers ally'd in blood,
Or sworn to that sweet sister-hood :
For health on Julia's cheek hath shed
Clarret, and creame commingled.
And those her lips doe now appeare
As beames of corrall, but more cleare.

10

His Sailing from Julia.

"Remora" (l. 4), the sea-lamprey, which of old was supposed to stop ships by fastening on to their bottoms. Hesperides.

Wᴴᴇɴ that day comes, whose evening sayes
    I'm gone
Unto that watrie desolation :
Devoutly to thy closet-gods then pray,
That my wing'd ship may meet no Remora.
Those deities which circum-walk the seas,
And look upon our dreadfull passages,
Will from all dangers re-deliver me,
For one drink-offering poured out by thee.
Mercie and truth live with thee ! and forbeare
In my short absence, to unsluce a teare :
But yet for loves-sake, let thy lips doe this,
Give my dead picture one engendring kisse :
Work that to life, and let me ever dwell
In thy remembrance, Julia. So farewell.

—∿∿∿—

His Request to Julia.

Hesperides.

Jᴜʟɪᴀ, if I chance to die
Ere I print my poetry ;
I most humbly thee desire
To commit it to the fire :
Better 'twere my book were dead,
Then to live not perfected.

11

If, deare Anthea. Hesperides.

IF, deare Anthea, my hard fate it be
To live some few-sad-howers after thee :
Thy sacred corse with odours I will burne ;
And with my lawrell crown thy golden vrne.
Then holding up, there, such religious things,
As were, time past, thy holy filitings :
Nere to thy reverend pitcher I will fall
Down dead for grief, and end my woes withall :
So three in one small plat of ground shall ly,
Anthea, Herrick, and his poetry.

—∿∿∿—

To Anthea. "Who may command him any thing." Hesperides.

BID me to live, and I will live
    Thy Protestant to be :
Or bid me love, and I will give
    A loving heart to thee.

A heart as soft, a heart as kind,
    A heart as sound and free,
As in the whole world thou canst find,
    That heart Ile give to thee.

Bid that heart stay, and it will stay,
    To honour thy decree :
Or bid it languish quite away,
    And't shall doe so for thee.

Herrick.

Bid me to weep, and I will weep,
  While I have eyes to see :
And having none, yet I will keep
  A heart to weep for thee.

Bid me despaire, and Ile despaire,
  Under that cypresse tree :
Or bid me die, and I will dare
  E'en Death, to die for thee.

Thou art my life, my love, my heart,
  The very eyes of me :
And hast command of every part,
  To live and die for thee.

—⁓⋀⋁⋀⁓—

To Daffadills.   Hesperides.

FAIRE Daffadills, we weep to see
  You haste away so soone :
As yet the early-rising sun
  Has not attain'd his noone.
     Stay, stay,
  Untill the hasting day
     Has run
  But to the Even-song ;
And, having pray'd together, we
  Will goe with you along.

We have short time to stay, as you,
  We have as short a spring ;
As quick a growth to meet decay,
  As you, or any thing.

Lyric Poems.

We die,
As your hours doe, and drie
Away,
Like to the summers raine ;
Or as the pearles of morning's dew
Ne'r to be found againe.

—ᴧᴧᴧᴧᴧ—

To Daisies, not
to Shut so   Hesperides.
soone.

Shut not so soon ; the dull-ey'd night
Ha's not as yet begunne
To make a seisure on the light,
Or to seale up the sun.

No marigolds yet closed are ;
No shadowes great appeare ;
Nor doth the early shepheards starre
Shine like a spangle here.

Stay but till my Julia close
Her life-begetting eye ;
And let the whole world then dispose
It selfe to live or dye.

—ᴧᴧᴧᴧᴧ—

14

The Night-piece.

To Julia.   Hesperides.

H ER eyes the glow-worme lend thee,
The shooting starres attend thee ;
  And the elves also,
  Whose little eyes glow,
Like the sparks of fire, befriend thee.

No Will-o'-th'-Wispe mis-light thee ;
Nor snake, or slow-worme bite thee :
  But on, on thy way
  Not making a stay,
Since ghost ther's none to affright thee.

Let not the darke thee cumber ;
What though the moon do's slumber?
  The starres of the night
  Will lend thee their light,
Like tapers cleare without number.

Then Julia let me wooe thee,
Thus, thus to come unto me :
  And when I shall meet
  Thy silv'ry feet,
My soule I'le poure into thee.

—\/\/\/\—

The Cheat of Cupid.

ONE silent night of late,
  When every creature rested,
Came one unto my gate,
  And knocking, me molested.

Who's that, said I, beats there,
  And troubles thus the sleepie?
Cast off, said he, all feare,
  And let not locks thus keep ye.

For I a Boy am, who
  By moonlesse nights have swerved
And all with showrs wet through,
  And e'en with cold half starved.

I pittifull arose,
  And soon a taper lighted ;
And did my selfe disclose
  Unto the lad benighted.

I saw he had a bow,
  And wings too, which did shiver ;
And looking down below,
  I spy'd he had a quiver.

16

Herrick.

I to my chimney's shine
   Brought him, as love professes,
And chaf'd his hands with mine,
   And dry'd his dropping tresses :

But when he felt him warm'd,
   Let's try this bow of ours,
And string, if they be harm'd,
   Said he, with these late showrs.

Forthwith his bow he bent,
   And wedded string and arrow,
And struck me that it went
   Quite through my heart and marrow.

Then laughing loud, he flew
   Away, and thus said flying,
Adieu, mine host, adieu,
   Ile leave thy heart a dying.

—◦◦◦◦—

The Bag of the Bee.

Hesperides.

About the sweet bag of a bee,
   Two Cupids fell at odds ;
And whose the pretty prize shu'd be,
   They vow'd to ask the gods.

Which Venus hearing, thither came,
   And for their boldness stript them :
And taking thence from each his flame ;
   With rods of mirtle whipt them.

Lyric Poems.

Which done, to still their wanton cries,
When quiet grown sh'ad seen them,
She kist, and wip'd thir dove-like eyes ;
And gave the bag between them.

—⋀⋁⋀—

The Wounded Cupid.

Song. Hesperides.

CUPID as he lay among
Roses, by a bee was stung.
Whereupon in anger flying
To his mother, said thus crying ;
Help ! O help ! your boy's a dying.
And why, my pretty lad, said she?
Then blubbering, replyed he,
A winged snake has bitten me,
Which country people call a bee.
At which she smil'd ; then with her hairs
And kisses drying up his tears :
Alas ! said she, my wag ! if this
Such a pernicious torment is :
Come tel me then, how great's the smart
Of those, thou woundest with thy dart !

—⋀⋁⋀—

18

Cupid Cupped. Hesperides.

As lately I a garland bound,
'Mongst roses, I there Cupid found :
I took him, put him in my cup,
And drunk with wine, I drank him up.
Hence then it is, that my poore brest
Co'd never since find any rest.

—∿∿∿—

Upon Cupid. Hesperides.

Love, like a gypsie, lately came ;
And did me much importune
To see my hand ; that by the same
He might fore-tell my fortune.

He saw my palme ; and then, said he,
I tell thee, by this score here ;
That thou, within few months, shalt be
The youthfull Prince D' Amour here.

I smil'd ; and bade him once more prove,
And by some crosse-line show it ;
That I co'd ne'r be Prince of Love,
Though here the princely poet.

The Captiv'd Bee.

As Julia once a slumb'ring lay,
It chanc't a bee did flie that way,
After a dew, or dew-like shower,
To tipple freely in a flower.
For some rich flower, he took the lip
Of Julia, and began to sip;
But when he felt he suckt from thence
Hony, and in the quintessence:
He drank so much he scarce co'd stir;
So Julia took the pilferer.
And thus surpriz'd, as filchers use,
He thus began himselfe t'excuse:
Sweet lady-flower, I never brought
Hither the least one theeving thought:
But taking those rare lips of yours
For some fresh, fragrant, luscious flowers;
I thought I might there take a taste,
Where so much sirrop ran at waste.
Besides, know this, I never sting
The flower that gives me nourishing:
But with a kisse, or thanks, doe pay
For honie, that I beare away.
This said, he laid his little scrip
Of hony, 'fore her ladiship:
And told her, as some tears did fall,
That, that he took, and that was all.
At which she smil'd; and bade him goe

20

And take his bag ; but this much know,
When next he came a pilfring so,
He sho'd from her full lips derive,
Hony enough to fill his hive.

—⁓⁓—

A Meditation
for his   Hesperides.
Mistresse.

You are a tulip seen to day,
But, dearest, of so short a stay ;
That where you grew, scarce man can say.

You are a lovely July-flower,
Yet one rude wind, or ruffling shower,
Will force you hence, and in an houre.

You are a sparkling rose i'th'bud,
Yet lost, ere that chast flesh and blood
Can shew where you or grew, or stood.

You are a full-spread faire-set vine,
And can with tendrills love intwine,
Yet dry'd, ere you distill your wine.

You are like balme inclosed, well,
In amber, or some chrystall shell,
Yet lost ere you transfuse your smell.

You are a dainty violet,
Yet wither'd, ere you can be set
Within the virgin's coronet.

You are the queen all flowers among,
But die you must, faire maid, ere long,
As he, the maker of this song.

—✳✳✳—

To the Water Nymphs, Drinking at the Fountain.

Hesperides.

Reach, with your whiter hands, to me,
    Some christall of the spring ;
And I, about the cup shall see
    Fresh lillies flourishing.

Or else sweet nimphs do you but this ;
    'To'th' glasse your lips encline ;
And I shall see by that one kisse,
    The water turn'd to wine.

—✳✳✳—

Pansies.

How Pansies or
Hearts ease came first.
Hesperides.

Frollick virgins once these were,
Over-loving, living here :
Being here their ends deny'd
Ranne for sweet-hearts mad, and dy'd.

22

Herrick.

Love in pittie of their teares,
And their losse in blooming yeares ;
For their restlesse here-spent houres,
Gave them hearts-ease turn'd to flow'rs.

—◁◁◁◁—

To Violets.

Welcome, maids of honour,
    You doe bring
    In the spring ;
And wait upon her.

She has virgins many,
    Fresh and faire ;
    Yet you are
More sweet then any.

Y'are the maiden posies,
    And so grac't,
    To be plac't,
'Fore damask roses.

Yet though thus respected,
    By and by
    Ye doe lie,
Poore girles, neglected.

To a Bed of Tulips.

Hesperides

Bright tulips, we do know,
You had your comming hither;
And fading-time do's show,
That ye must quickly wither.

Your sister-hoods may stay,
And smile here for your houre;
But dye ye must away:
Even as the meanest flower.

Come, virgins, then, and see
Your frailties; and bemone ye;
For lost like these, 'twill be,
As time had never known ye.

—⁓⁓⁓—

To the Virgins.

"To make much of Time." Hesperides.

Gather ye rose-buds while ye may,
    Old Time is still a-flying:
And this same flower that smiles to-day,
    To morrow will be dying.

The glorious lamp of heaven, the sun,
    The higher he's a getting;
The sooner will his race be run,
    And neerer he's to setting.

24

Herrick.

That age is best, which is the first,
    When youth and blood are warmer ;
But being spent, the worse, and worst
    Times still succeed the former.

Then be not coy, but use your time ;
    And while ye may, goe marry :
For having lost but once your prime,
    You may for ever tarry.

—\/\/\/\—

Why Flowers change Colour.   Hesperides.

THESE fresh beauties, we can prove,
Once were virgins sick of love,
Turn'd to flowers. Still in some
Colours goe, and colours come.

—\/\/\/\—

To Carnations.   A Song. Hesperides.

STAY while ye will, or goe ;
    And leave no scent behind ye :
Yet trust me, I shall know
    The place, where I may find ye :

Within my Lucia's cheek,
    Whose livery ye weare,
Play ye at hide or seek,
    I'm sure to find ye there.

25

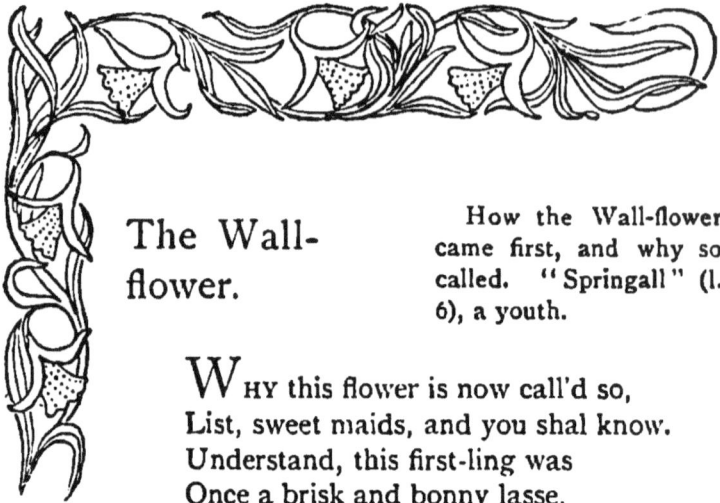

The Wall-flower.

How the Wall-flower came first, and why so called. "Springall" (l. 6), a youth.

WHY this flower is now call'd so,
List, sweet maids, and you shal know.
Understand, this first-ling was
Once a brisk and bonny lasse,
Kept as close as Danae was :
Who a sprightly springall lov'd,
And to have it fully prov'd,
Up she got upon a wall,
Tempting down to slide withall :
But the silken twist unty'd,
So she fell, and bruis'd, she dy'd.
Love, in pitty of the deed,
And her loving-lucklesse speed,
Turn'd her to this plant, we call
Now, The Flower of the Wall.

—WWW—

How Roses came Red.

Hesperides

ROSES at first were white,
  Till they co'd not agree,
Whether my Sapho's breast,
  Or they more white sho'd be.

26

Herrick.

But being vanquisht quite,
    A blush their cheeks bespred ;
Since which, beleeve the rest,
    The roses first came red.

—◊◊◊—

How Violets came Blew.

Love on a day, wise poets tell,
    Some time in wrangling spent,
Whether the violets sho'd excell,
    Or she, in sweetest scent.

But Venus having lost the day,
    Poore girles, she fell on you ;
And beat ye so, as some dare say,
    Her blowes did make ye blew.

—◊◊◊—

How Lillies came White.

Hesperides.

White though ye be ; yet, lillies, know
From the first ye were not so :
        But Ile tell ye
        What befell ye ;
Cupid and his mother lay
In a cloud ; where both did play,

27

He with his pretty finger prest
The rubie niplet of her breast ;
Out of the which, the creame of light,
    Like to a dew,
    Fell downe on you,
    And made ye white.

—◇◇◇—

To Primroses: "Fill'd with Morning-Dew." Hesperides.

WHY doe ye weep, sweet babes? can tears
    Speak griefe in you,
    Who were but borne
    Just as the modest morne
    Teem'd her refreshing dew ?
Alas, you have not known that shower,
    That marres a flower ;
    Nor felt th'unkind
    Breath of a blasting wind ;
    Nor are ye worne with yeares ;
    Or warpt, as we,
    Who think it strange to see,
Such pretty flowers, like to orphans young,
To speak by teares, before ye have a tongue.

Speak, whimp'ring younglings, and make known
    The reason, why
    Ye droop, and weep ;
    Is it for want of sleep ?
    Or childish lullabie ?

Herrick.

Or that ye have not seen as yet
    The violet?
    Or brought a kisse
From that sweet-heart, to this?
    No, no, this sorrow shown
        By your teares shed,
    Wo'd have this lecture read,
That things of greatest, so of meanest worth,
Conceiv'd with grief are, and with tears brought
    forth.

—◡◡◡—

To Blossoms.

Faire pledges of a fruitfull tree,
    Why do yee fall so fast?
    Your date is not so past;
But you may stay yet here a while,
    To blush and gently smile;
        And go at last.

What, were yee borne to be
    An houre or half's delight;
    And so to bid goodnight?
'Twas pitie Nature brought yee forth
    Meerly to shew your worth,
        And lose you quite.

But you are lovely leaves, where we
    May read how soon things have
    Their end, though ne'r so brave:
And after they have shown their pride,
    Like you a while: they glide
        Into the grave.

29

To Meddowes. Hesperides.

Yᴇ have been fresh and green,
  Ye have been fill'd with flowers :
And ye the walks have been
  Where maids have spent their houres.

You have beheld, how they
  With wicker arks did come
To kisse, and beare away
  The richer couslips home.

Y'ave heard them sweetly sing,
  And seen them in a round :
Each virgin, like a Spring,
  With hony-succles crown'd.

But now, we see, none here,
  Whose silv'rie feet did tread.
And with dishevell'd haire,
  Adorn'd this smoother mead.

Like unthrifts, having spent
  Your stock, and needy grown,
Y'are left here to lament
  Your poore estates, alone.

Herrick.

The Mad Maid's Song.

Good morrow to the day so fair ;
Good morning, sir, to you :
Good morrow to mine own torn hair
Bedabled with the dew.

Good morning to this primrose too ;
Good morrow to each maid ;
That will with flowers the tomb bestrew,
Wherein my Love is laid.

Ah ! woe is mee, woe, woe is me,
Alack and welladay !
For pitty, sir, find out that bee,
Which bore my Love away.

I'le seek him in your bonnet brave ;
Ile seek him in your eyes ;
Nay, now I think th'ave made his grave
I' th'bed of strawburies.

Ile seek him there ; I know, ere this,
The cold, cold earth doth shake him ;
But I will go, or send a kisse
By you, sir, to awake him.

Pray hurt him not ; though he be dead,
He knowes well who do love him,
And who with green-turfes reare his head,
And who do rudely move him.

He's soft and tender (pray take heed)
With bands of cow-slips bind him ;
And bring him home ; but 'tis decreed,
That I shall never find him.

—ᴡᴡ—

To Musique :   " To becalme his fever."
                Hesperides.

CHARM me asleep, and melt me so
With thy delicious numbers ;
That being ravisht, hence I goe
Away in easie slumbers.
　　Ease my sick head,
　　And make my bed,
Thou power that canst sever
　　From me this ill :
　　And quickly still :
　　Though thou not kill
　　　My fever.

Thou sweetly canst convert the same
From a consuming fire,
Into a gentle-licking flame,
And make it thus expire.
　　Then make me weep
　　My paines asleep ;
And give me such reposes,
　　That I, poore I,
　　May think, thereby,
　　I live and die
　　　'Mongst roses.

32

Fall on me like a silent dew,
  Or like those maiden showrs,
Which, by the peepe of day, doe strew
  A baptime o're the flowers.
    Melt, melt my paines,
    With thy soft straines ;
  That having ease me given,
    With full delight,
    I leave this light ;
  And take my flight
    For heaven.

—∿∿—

His Poetrie his Pillar.

Hesperides.

Onely a little more
  I have to write,
    Then Ile give o're,
And bid the world good-night.

'Tis but a flying minute,
  That I must stay,
    Or linger in it ;
And then I must away.

O Time that cut'st down all
  And scarce leav'st here
    Memoriall
Of any men that were.

10 C   33

How many lye forgot
    In vaults beneath?
    And piece-meale rot
Without a fame in death?

Behold this living stone,
    I reare for me,
    Ne'r to be thrown
Downe, envious Time, by thee.

Pillars let some set up,
    If so they please,
    ·Here is my hope,
And my pyramides.

—ᴡᴡᴠᴡ—

Divination by a Daffadill.   Hesperides.

WHEN a daffadill I see,
Hanging down his head t'wards me;
Guesse I may, what I must be:
First, I shall decline my head;
Secondly, I shall be dead;
Lastly, safely buryed.

—ᴡᴡᴠᴡ—

The Olive-Branch.

Sadly I walkt within the field,
To see what comfort it wo'd yeeld :
And as I went my private way,
An olive-branch before me lay :
And seeing it, I made a stay.
And took it up, and view'd it ; then
Kissing the omen, said Amen :
Be, be it so, and let this be
A divination unto me :
That in short time my woes shall cease ;
And love shall crown my end with peace.

—ᴡᴡᴡ—

To Julia.

The saints-bell calls ; and, Julia, I must read
The proper lessons for the saints now dead :
To grace which service, Julia, there shall be
One Holy Collect, said or sung for thee.
Dead when thou art, deare Julia, thou shalt
        have
A trentall sung by virgins o're thy grave :
Meane time we two will sing the dirge of these ;
Who dead, deserve our best remembrances.

35

The Plaudite. Or End of Life. Hesperides.

IF after rude and boystrous seas,
My wearyed pinnace here finds ease :
If so it be I've gain'd the shore
With safety of a faithful ore :
If having run my barque on ground,
Ye see the aged vessell crown'd :
What's to be done? but on the sands
Ye dance, and sing, and now clap hands.
The first act's doubtfull, but we say,
It is the last commends the play.

—ɯʌʌ—

To Sylvia. Hesperides.

I AM holy, while I stand
Circum-crost by thy pure hand ;
But when that is gone ; again,
I, as others, am prophane.

—ɯʌʌ—

My Muse in Meads. "To Mistresse Katherine Bradshaw, the lovely, that crowned him with Laurel." Hesperides.

MY Muse in meads has spent her many
    houres,
Sitting, and sorting severall sorts of flowers,
To make for others garlands ; and to set
On many a head here, many a coronet :

36

Herrick.

But, amongst all encircled here, not one
Gave her a day of coronation ;
Till you, sweet mistresse, came and enterwove
A laurel for her, ever young as love,
You first of al crown'd her ; she must of due,
Render for that, a crowne of life to you.

—ᴧᴧᴧ—

His Lacrime. Or "Mirth turn'd to Mourning." Hesperides.

C<small>ALL</small> me no more,
As heretofore,
The musick of a feast ;
Since now, alas,
The mirth, that was
In me, is dead or ceast.

Before I went
To banishment
Into the loathed west ;
I co'd rehearse
A lyrick verse,
And speak it with the best.

But time, ai me,
Has laid, I see,
My organ fast asleep ;
And turn'd my voice
Into the noise
Of those that sit and weep.

37

On Himself.

A WEARIED pilgrim, I have wandred here
Twice five and twenty, bate me but one yeer ;
Long I have lasted in this world ; 'tis true,
But yet those yeers that I have liv'd, but few.
Who by his gray haires, doth his lusters tell,
Lives not those yeers, but he that lives them
    well.
One man has reatch't his sixty yeers, but he
Of all those three-score, has not liv'd halfe
    three :
He lives, who lives to virtue : men who cast
Their ends for pleasure, do not live, but last.

—◁◁◁—

The Dreame.

BY dream I saw, one of the three
Sisters of Fate appeare to me.
Close to my beds side she did stand
Shewing me there a fire brand ;
She told me too, as that did spend,
So drew my life unto an end.
Three quarters were consum'd of it ;
Onely remaind a little bit,
Which will be burnt up by and by,
Then Julia weep, for I must dy.

To Anthea. Hesperides.

Now is the time, when all the lights wax dim;
And thou, Anthea, must withdraw from him
Who was thy servant. Dearest, bury me
Under that holy-oke, or gospel-tree :
Where, though thou see'st not, thou may'st
    think upon
Me, when thou yeerly go'st procession :
Or for mine honour, lay me in that tombe
In which thy sacred reliques shall have roome
For my embalming, sweetest, there will be
No spices wanting, when I'm laid by thee.

—ᴧᴧ/ᴧᴧ—

His Embalming. To Julia. Hesperides.

For my embalming, Julia, do but this,
Give thou my lips but their supreamest kiss :
Or else trans-fuse thy breath into the chest,
Where my small reliques must for ever rest :
That breath the balm, the myrrh, the nard
    shal be,
To give an incorruption unto me.

—ᴧᴧ/ᴧᴧ—

To Robin Red-breast.

LAID out for dead, let thy last kindnesse be
With leaves and mosse-work for to cover me :
And while the wood-nimphs my cold corps
    inter,
Sing thou my dirge, sweet-warbling chorister !
For epitaph, in foliage, next write this,
   Here, here the tomb of Robin Herrick is.

—wVVw—

The Bracelet to Julia.

WHY I tye about thy wrist,
Julia, this my silken twist ;
For what other reason is't,
But to shew thee how in part,
Thou my pretty captive art?
But thy bondslave is my heart :
'Tis but silke that bindeth thee,
Knap the thread, and thou art free :
But 'tis otherwise with me ;
I am bound, and fast bound so,
That from thee I cannot go,
If I co'd, I wo'd not so.

On Julia's Breath.

Hesperides.

Breathe, Julia, breathe, and Ile protest,
    Nay more, Ile deeply sweare,
That all the spices of the East
    Are circumfused there.

—⋙⋘—

Upon his Julia.

Hesperides.

Will ye heare, what I can say
Briefly of my Julia?
Black and rowling is her eye,
Double chinn'd, and forehead high :
Lips she has, all rubie red,
Cheeks like creame enclarited :
And a nose that is the grace
And proscenium of her face.
So that we may guesse by these,
The other parts will richly please.

—⋙⋘—

A Short Hymne to Venus.

Hesperides.

GODDESSE, I do love a girle
Rubie-lipt, and tooth'd with pearl :
If so be, I may but prove
Luckie in this maide I love :
I will promise there shall be
Mirtles offer'd up to thee.

—◦◦◦—

The Kisse.

A dialogue. Hes-
perides.

1. AMONG thy fancies, tell me this
What is the thing we call a kisse?
2. I shall resolve ye, what it is.

It is a creature born and bred
Between the lips, all cherrie-red,
By love and warme desires fed,
Chor. And makes more soft the bridall bed.

2. It is an active flame, that flies,
First, to the babies of the eyes ;
And charmes them there with lullabies ;
Chor. And stils the bride too, when she cries.

2. Then to the chin, the cheek, the eare,
It frisks, and flyes, now here, now there,
'Tis now farre off, and then tis nere ;
Chor. And here, and there, and every where

42

Herrick.

1. Has it a speaking virtue ? 2. Yes.
1. How speaks it, say ? 2. Do you but this,
    Part your joyn'd lips, then speaks your
      kisse ;
Chor. And this love's sweetest language is.

1. Has it a body? 2. I, and wings,
    With thousand rare encolourings :
    And as it flyes, it gently sings,
Chor. Love, honie yeelds ; but never stings.

—vVVv—

To his Mistresse.

Objecting to him neither
Toying or Talking. Hes-
perides.

You say I love not, 'cause I doe not play
Still with your curles, and kisse the time away
You blame me too, because I cann't devise
Some sport, to please those babies in your eyes :
By loves religion, I must here confesse it,
The most I love, when I the least expresse it.
Small griefs find tongues : full casques are ever
    found
To give, if any, yet but little sound.
Deep waters noyse-lesse are ; and this we know,
That chiding streams betray small depth below.
So when love speechlesse is she doth expresse
A depth in love, and that depth, bottomlesse.
Now since my love is tougue-lesse, know me
    such,
Who speak but little, 'cause I love so much.

43

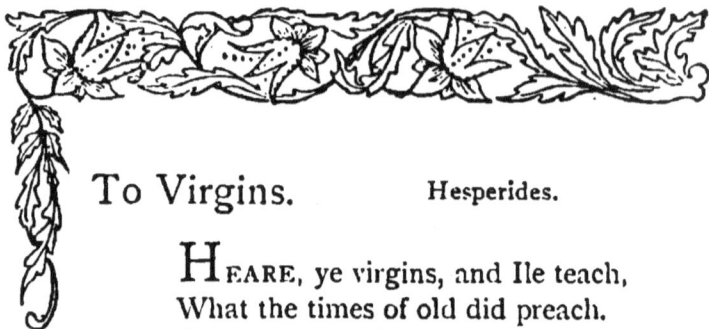

To Virgins. Hesperides.

HEARE, ye virgins, and Ile teach,
What the times of old did preach.
Rosamond was in a bower
Kept, as Danae in a tower :
But yet Love, who subtile is,
Crept to that, and came to this.
But ye lockt up like to these,
Or the rich Hesperides ;
Or those babies in your eyes,
In their christall nunneries ;
Notwithstanding Love will win,
Or else force a passage in :
And as coy be, as you can,
Gifts will get ye, or the man.

—◊◊◊—

Chop-Cherry. Hesperides.

THOU gav'st me leave to kisse ;
Thou gav'st me leave to wooe ;
Thou mad'st me thinke by this,
And that, thou lov'dst me too.

But I shall ne'r forget,
How for to make thee merry ;
Thou mad'st me chop, but yet,
Another snapt the cherry.

Herrick.

I call and I call.

Hesperides

I call, I call : who doe ye call?
The maids to catch this cowslip-ball :
But since these cowslips fading be,
Troth, leave the flowers, and maids, take me.
Yet, if that neither you will doe,
Speak but the word, and Ile take you.

—∿∿∿—

A Lyrick to Mirth.

Hesperides.

WHILE the milder fates consent,
Let's enjoy our merryment :
Drink, and dance, and pipe, and play ;
Kisse our dollies night and day :
Crown'd with clusters of the vine ;
Let us sit, and quaffe our wine.
Call on Bacchus ; chaunt his praise ;
Shake the thyrse, and bite the bayes :
Rouze Anacreon from the dead ;
And return him drunk to bed :
Sing o're Horace ; for ere long
Death will come and mar the song :
Then shall Wilson and Gotiere
Never sing, or play more here.

45

To the Western Wind.

Hesperides.

Sweet western wind, whose luck it is,
  Made rivall with the aire,
To give Perenna's lip a kisse,
  And fan her wanton haire.

Bring me but one, Ile promise thee,
  Instead of common showers,
Thy wings shall be embalm'd by me,
  And all beset with flowers.

—◦◦◦—

The Bleeding Hand :

Or, The Sprig of Eg-
lantine given to a Maid.
Hesperides.

From this bleeding hand of mine,
Take this sprig of eglantine.
Which, though sweet unto your smell,
Yet the fretfull bryar will tell,
Ile who plucks the sweets shall prove
Many thorns to be in love.

—◦◦◦—

46

Herrick.

The Suspition :

Upon his overmuch familiarity with a gentle-woman. Hesperides. (III.) " Fame's black lips " (last line), " Fame was painted with black lips, puffing at a trumpet, like so."

AND must we part, because some say,
Loud is our love, and loose our play,
And more then well becomes the day ?
Alas for pitty ! and for us
Most innocent, and injur'd thus.
Had we kept close, or play'd within,
Suspition now had been the sinne,
And shame had follow'd long ere this,
T'ave plagu'd, what now unpunisht is.
But we as fearlesse of the sunne,
As faultlesse ; will not wish undone,
What now is done : since *where no sin*
Unbolts the doore, no shame comes in.
Then, comely and most fragrant maid,
Be you more warie, then afraid
Of these reports ; because you see
The fairest most suspected be.
The common formes have no one eye,
Or care of burning jealousie
To follow them : but chiefly, where
Love makes the cheek, and chin a sphere
To dance and play in : trust me, there
Suspicion questions every haire.
Come, you are faire ; and sho'd be seen
While you are in your sprightfull green :

47

And what though you had been embrac't
By me, were you for that unchast?
No, no, no more then is yond' moone,
Which shining in her perfect noone;
In all that great and glorious light,
Continues cold, as is the night.
Then, beauteous maid, you may retire;
And as for me, my chast desire
Shall move t'wards you; although I see
Your face no more: so live you free
From Fame's black lips, as you from me.

—\/\/\/\—

To the Lark. Hesperides.

Good speed, for I this day
　　Betimes my mattens say:
　　Because I doe
　　Begin to wooe:
　　Sweet singing lark,
　　Be thou the clark,
　　And know thy when
　　To say, Amen.
　　And if I prove
　　Blest in my love;
　　Then thou shalt be
　　High-priest to me,
　　At my returne,
　　To incense burne;
And so to solemnize
Love's, and my sacrifice.

48

The Bubble. A Song. Hesperides.

To my revenge, and to her desp'rate feares,
Flie, thou made bubble of my sighs and tears.
In the wild aire, when thou hast rowl'd about,
And, like a blasting planet, found her out ;
Stoop, mount, passe by to take her eye, then
  glare
Like to a dreadfull comet in the aire :
Next, when thou dost perceive her fixed sight,
For thy revenge to be most opposite ;
Then like a globe, or ball of wild-fire, flie,
And break thy self in shivers on her eye.

—Ʌ/\/\ᴡ—

Upon Electra. Hesperides.

When out of bed my love doth spring,
'*Tis but as day a kindling:*
But when she's up and fully drest,
'Tis then *broad day throughout the east.*

—Ʌ/\/\ᴡ—

Upon a Black Twist : " Rounding the arme of the Countesse of Carlile." Hesperides.

I saw about her spotlesse wrist,
Of blackest silk, a curious twist ;
Which, circumvolving gently, there
Enthrall'd her arme, as prisoner.

Lyric Poems.

Dark was the jayle ; but as if light
Had met t'engender with the night ;
Or so, as darknesse made a stay
To shew at once, both night and day.
I fancie more ! but if there be
Such freedome in captivity ;
I beg of Love, that never I
May in like chains of darknesse lie.

—◊◊◊—

Upon a Flie.

"Phil," a pet bird ; in this instance stuffed and put in a glass case. (Compare Sidney.) Hesperides.

A golden flie once shew'd to me,
Clos'd in a box of yvorie :
Where both seem'd proud ; the flie to have
His buriall in an yvorie grave :
The yvorie tooke state to hold
A corps as bright as burnisht gold.
One fate had both ; both equall grace ;
The buried, and the burying-place.
Not Virgils gnat, to whom the spring
All flowers sent to'is burying.
Not Marshalls bee, which in a bead
Of amber quick was buried.
Nor that fine worme that do's interre
Her selfe i'th' silken sepulchre.
Nor my rare Phil, that lately was
With lillies tomb'd up in a glasse ;
More honour had, then this same flie ;
Dead, and closed up in yvorie.

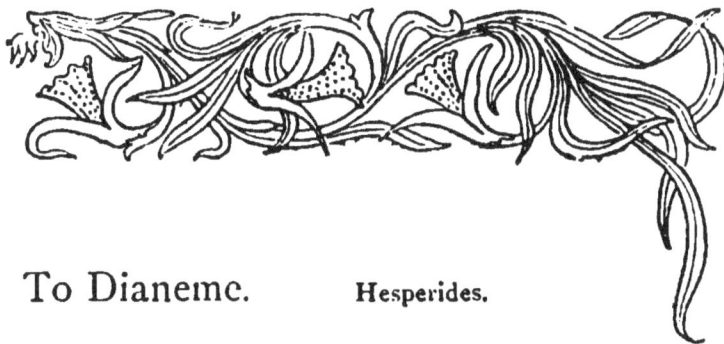

To Dianeme. Hesperides.

I.

Sweet, be not proud of those two eyes,
Which star-like sparkle in their skies :
Nor be you proud, that you can see
All hearts your captives ; yours, yet free :
Be you not proud of that rich haire,
Which wantons with the love-sick aire :
When as that rubie, which you weare,
Sunk from the tip of your soft eare,
Will last to be a precious stone,
When all your world of beautie's gone.

II.

I co'd but see thee yesterday
  Stung by a fretfull bee ;
And I the javelin suckt away,
  And heal'd the wound in thee.

A thousand thorns, and bryars & stings,
  I have in my poore brest ;
Yet ne'r can see that salve which brings
  My passions any rest.

51

Lyric Poems.

As Love shall helpe me, I admire
  How thou canst sit and smile,
To see me bleed, and not desire
  To stench the blood the while.

If thou compos'd of gentle mould
  Art so unkind to me ;
What dismall stories will be told
  Of those that cruell be ?

III.

Deare, though to part it be a hell,
Yet, Dianeme, now farewell :
Thy frown, last night, did bid me goe ;
But whither, onely grief do's know.
I doe beseech thee, ere we part,
(If mercifull, as faire thou art ;
Or else desir'st that maids sho'd tell
Thy pitty by Loves-chronicle)
O Dianeme, rather kill
Me, then to make me languish stil !
'Tis cruelty in thee to'th'height,
Thus, thus to wound, not kill out-right :
Yet there's a way found, if thou please,
By sudden death to give me ease :
And thus devis'd, doe thou but this
Bequeath to me one parting kisse :
So sup'rabundant joy shall be
The executioner of me.

—⌇⌇⌇—

Herrick.

The Vision to Electra.

Hesperides.

I DREAM'D we both were in a bed
Of roses, almost smothered :
The warmth and sweetnes had me there
Made lovingly familiar ;
But that I heard thy sweet breath say,
Faults done by night, will blush by day :
I kist thee panting, and I call
Night to the record ! that was all.
But ah ! if empty dreames so please,
Love, give me more such nights as these.

—⋀⋁⋀⋁—

The Showre of Blossomes.

Hesperides.

LOVE in a showre of blossomes came
Down, and halfe drown'd me with the same :
The blooms that fell were white and red ;
But with such sweets commingled,
As whether, this, I cannot tell
My sight was pleas'd more, or my smell :
But true it was, as I rowl'd there,
Without a thought of hurt, or feare ;
Love turn'd himselfe into a bee,
And with his javelin wounded me :

53

From which mishap this use I make,
Where most sweets are, there lyes a snake :
Kisses and favours are sweet things ;
But those have thorns, and these have stings.

—◌◌◌—

How his Soule came Ensnared.   Hesperides.

My soule would one day goe and seeke
For roses, and in Julia's cheeke
A richess of those sweets she found,
As in an other Rosamond.
But gathering roses as she was ;
Not knowing what would come to passe,
It chanst a ringlet of her haire,
Caught my poore soule, as in a snare :
Which ever since has been in thrall ;
Yet freedome, shee enjoyes withall.

—◌◌◌—

Upon Love.   Hesperides.

Love brought me to a silent grove,
    And shew'd me there a tree,
Where some had hang'd themselves for love,
    And gave a twist to me.

54

Herrick.

The halter was of silk, and gold,
    That he reacht forth unto me :
No otherwise, then if he would
    By dainty things undo me.

He bade me then that neck-lace use ;
    And told me too, he maketh
A glorious end by such a noose,
    His death for love that taketh.

'Twas but a dream ; but had I been
    There really alone ;
My desp'rate feares, in love, had seen
    Mine execution.

—ʌ/\/\ʌ—

To Julia, in her Dawn, or Day- breake.

By the next kindling of the day
    My Julia thou shalt see,
Ere Ave-Mary thou canst say
    Ile come and visit thee.

Yet ere thou counsel'st with thy glasse,
    Appeare thou to mine eyes
As smooth, and nak't, as she that was
    The prime of paradice.

If blush thou must, then blush thou through
   A lawn, that thou may'st looke
As purest pearles, or pebles do
   When peeping through a brooke.

As lillies shrin'd in christall, so
   Do thou to me appeare ;
Or damask roses when they grow
   To sweet acquaintance there.

—ᴡᴠᴠᴠᴡ—

The Trans-figuration.   Hesperides.

Immortall clothing I put on,
So soone as Julia I am gon
To mine eternall mansion.

Thou, thou art here, to humane sight
Cloth'd all with incorrupted light ;
But yet how more admir'dly bright

Wilt thou appear, when thou art set
In thy refulgent thronelet,
That shin'st thus in thy counterfeit ?

—ᴡᴠᴠᴠᴡ—

Crutches.   Hesperides.

Thou seest me, Lucia, this year droope,
Three zodiaks fill'd more I shall stoope ;
Let crutches then provided be
To shore up my debilitie.

Herrick.

Then while thou laugh'st ; Ile, sighing, crie,
A ruine underpropt am I :
Do'n will I then my beadsmans gown,
And when so feeble I am grown,
As my weake shoulders cannot beare
The burden of a grashopper :
Yet with the bench of aged sires,
When I and they keep tearmly fires ;
With my weake voice I'le sing, or say
Some odes I made of Lucia :
Then will I heave my wither'd hand
To Jove the mighty for to stand
Thy faithfull friend, and to poure downe
Upon thee many a benizon.

—◁◁◁—

His Teares to Thamasis.

I SEND, I send here my supremest kiss
To thee, my silver-footed Thamasis.
No more shall I reiterate thy strand,
Whereon so many stately structures stand :
Nor in the summers sweeter evenings go,
To bath in thee, as thousand others doe,
No more shall I a long thy christall glide,
In barge, with boughes and rushes beautifi'd,
With soft-smooth virgins, for our chast disport,
To Richmond, Kingstone, and to Hampton-
    Court :
Never againe shall I with finnie-ore
Put from, or draw unto the faithfull shore :

And landing here, or safely landing there,
Make way to my beloved Westminster :
Or to the Golden-cheap-side, where the earth
Of Julia Herrick gave to me my birth.
May all clean nimphs and curious water dames,
With swan-like-state, flote up and down thy
   streams :
No drought upon thy wanton waters fall
To make them leane, and languishing at all.
No ruffling winds come hither to discease
Thy pure, and silver-wristed Naides.
Keep up your state, ye streams; and as ye
   spring,
Never make sick your banks by surfeiting.
Grow young with tydes, and though I see ye
   never,
Receive this vow, so fare-ye-well for ever.

—◁◆▷—

His last Request to Julia.

Hesperides.

I HAVE been wanton, and too bold I feare,
To chafe o're much the virgins cheek or eare :
Beg for my pardon, Julia ; *He doth winne*
Grace with the gods, who's sorry for his sinne.
That done, my Julia, dearest Julia, come,
And go with me to chuse my buriall roome :
My fates are ended ; when thy Herrick dyes,
Claspe thou his book, then close thou up his
   eyes.

Herrick.

To Julia. Hesperides.

JULIA, when thy Herrick dies,
Close thou up thy poets eyes :
And his last breath, let it be
Taken in by none but thee.

—⁓⋀⋀⋁⋎⁓—

Upon Julia's Clothes. Hesperides.

WHEN as in silks my Julia goes,
Then, then (me thinks) how sweetly flowes
That liquefaction of her clothes.

Next, when I cast mine eyes and see
That brave vibration each way free ;
O how that glittering taketh me !

—⁓⋀⋀⋁⋎⁓—

Delight in Disorder. Hesperides.

A SWEET disorder in the dresse
Kindles in cloathes a wantonnesse :
A lawne about the shoulders thrown
Into a fine distraction :

57

An erring lace, which here and there
Enthralls the crimson stomacher :
A cuffe neglectfull, and thereby
Ribbands to flow confusedly :
A winning wave (deserving note)
In the tempestuous petticote ;
A careless shooe-string, in whose tye
I see a wilde civility :
Doe more bewitch me, then when art
Is too precise in every part.

—◦◦◦◦—

The Carkanet.

The Carkanet was a necklet of gold filagree and, in this case, fine jet work. Hesperides.

INSTEAD of orient pearls, of jet
I sent my love a Carkanet :
About her spotlesse neck she knit
The lace, to honour me, or it :
Then think how wrapt was I to see
My jet t'enthrall such ivorie.

—◦◦◦◦—

Julia's Petticoat.

"Pounc't" (l. 9), Dusted, sprinkled. Hesperides.

THY azure robe, I did behold,
As ayrie as the leaves of gold ;
Which erring here, and wandring there,
Pleas'd with transgression ev'ry where :

63

Herrick.

Sometimes 'two'd pant, and sigh, and heave,
As if to stir it scarce had leave :
But having got it ; thereupon,
'Two'd make a brave expansion.
And pounc't with stars, it shew'd to me
Like a celestiall canopie.
Sometimes 'two'd blaze, and then abate,
Like to a flame growne moderate :
Sometimes away 'two'd wildly fling ;
Then to thy thighs so closely cling,
That some conceit did melt me downe,
As lovers fall into a swoone :
And all confus'd, I there did lie
Drown'd in delights ; but co'd not die.
That leading cloud, I follow'd still,
Hoping t'ave seene of it my fill ;
But ah ! I co'd not : sho'd it move
To life eternal, I co'd love.

The Eye.

"Lations" (l. 4), Planetary relations. "Chamlets" (l. 11), camlets. Hesperides.

MAKE me a heaven ; and make me there
Many a lesse and greater spheare.
Make me the straight, and oblique lines ;
The motions, lations, and the signes.
Make me a chariot, and a sun ;
And let them through a zodiac run :
Next, place me zones, and tropicks there ;
With all the seasons of the yeare.
Make me a sun-set ; and a night :
And then present the mornings-light
Cloath'd in her chamlets of delight.
To these, make clouds to poure downe raine ;
With weather foule, then faire againe.
And when, wise artist, that thou hast,
With all that can be, this heaven grac't ;
Ah ! what is then this curious skie,
But onely my Corinna's eye ?

—ᴧᴧᴧ—

The Apron of Flowers.

Hesperides.

To gather flowers Sappha went
And homeward she did bring
Within her lawnie continent,
The treasure of the spring.

Herrick.

She smiling blusht, and blushing smil'd,
  And sweetly blushing thus,
She lookt as she'd been got with child
  By young Favonius.

Her apron gave (as she did passe)
  An odor more divine,
More pleasing too, then ever was
  The lap of Proserpine.

—∿∿—

Disswasions from Idlenesse.

Hesperides.

Cynthius pluck ye by the eare,
That ye may good doctrine heare.
Play not with the maiden-haire ;
For each ringlet there's a snare.
Cheek, and eye, and lip, and chin ;
These are traps to take fooles in.
Armes, and hands, and all parts else,
Are but toiles, or manicles
Set on purpose to enthrall
Men, but slothfulls most of all.
Live employ'd, and so live free
From these fetters ; like to me
Who have found, and still can prove,
The lazie man the most doth love.

—∿∿—

The Sadnesse of Things :

"For Sapho's Sick-
nesse." Hesperides.

LILLIES will languish ; violets look ill ;
Sickly the prim-rose ; pale the daffadill :
That gallant tulip will hang down his head,
Like to a virgin newly ravished.
Pansies will weep ; and marigolds will wither ;
And keep a fast, and funerall together,
If Sapho droop ; daisies will open never,
But bid good-night, and close their lids for ever.

—〰〰—

The Lost Shepardesse.

"Mrs Eliz. Wheeler,
under the name of the
Lost Shepardesse." Hes-
perides.

AMONG the mirtles, as I walkt,
Love and my sighs thus intertalkt :
Tell me, said I, in deep distresse,
Where I may find my shepardesse.
Thou foole, said Love, know'st thou not this ?
In every thing that's sweet, she is.
In yond' carnation goe and seek,
There thou shalt find her lip and cheek :
In that ennamel'd pansie by,
There thou shalt have her curious eye :

Herrick.

In bloome of peach, and roses bud,
There waves the streamer of her blood.
'Tis true, said I, and thereupon
I went to pluck them one by one,
To make of parts an union ;
But on a sudden all were gone.
At which I stopt ; said Love, these be
The true resemblances of thee ;
For as these flowers, thy joyes must die,
And in the turning of an eye ;
And all thy hopes of her must wither,
Like those short sweets ere knit together.

—ᏙᎳᏙ—

Corinna's Going a Maying.

"The god unshorne"
(l. 2), Apollo. Hesper-
ides.

GET up, get up for shame, the blooming
    morne
    Upon her wings presents the god unshorne.
    See how Aurora throwes her faire
    Fresh-quilted colours through the aire :
    Get up, sweet Slug-a-bed, and see
    The dew-bespangling herbe and tree
Each flower has wept, and bow'd toward the
    east,
Above an houre since ; yet you not drest,
    Nay ! not so much as out of bed ?
    When all the birds have mattens seyd,

Lyric Poems.

And sung their thankfull hymnes : 'tis sin,
Nay, profanation to keep in,
When as a thousand virgins on this day,
Spring, sooner then the lark, to fetch in May.

Rise ; and put on your foliage, and be seene
To come forth, like the Spring-time, fresh and
    greene ;
  And sweet as Flora. Take no care
  For jewels for your gowne, or haire :
  Feare not ; the leaves will strew
  Gemms in abundance upon you :
Besides, the childhood of the day has kept,
Against you come, some orient pearls unwept :
  Come, and receive them while the light
  Hangs on the dew-locks of the night :
  And Titan on the eastern hill
  Retires himselfe, or else stands still
Til you come forth.   Wash, dresse, be briefe
    in praying :
Few beads are best, when once we goe a
    Maying.

Come, my Corinna, come ; and comming,
    marke
How each field turns a street ; each street a
    parke
  Made green, and trimm'd with trees : see
    how
  Devotion gives each house a bough,
  Or branch : each porch, each doore, ere this,
  An arke a tabernacle is
Made up of white-thorn neatly enterwove ;
As if here were those cooler shades of love.

Herrick.

Can such delights be in the street,
And open fields, and we not see't?
Come, we'll abroad; and let's obay
The proclamation made for May:
And sin no more, as we have done by staying;
But, my Corinna, come, let's goe a Maying.

There's not a budding boy, or girle, this day,
But is got up, and gone to bring in May.
    A deale of youth, ere this, is come
    Back, and with White-thorn laden home.
    Some have dispatcht their cakes and
        creame,
    Before that we have left to dreame:
And some have wept, and woo'd, and plighted
        troth,
And chose their priest, ere we can cast off sloth:
    Many a green-gown has been given;
    Many a kisse, both odde and even:
    Many a glance too has been sent
    From out the eye, love's firmament:
Many a jest told of the keyes betraying
That night, and locks pickt, yet w'are not a
        Maying.

Come, let us goe, while we are in our prime;
And take the harmlesse follie of the time.
    We shall grow old apace, and die
    Before we know our liberty.
    Our life is short; and our dayes run
    As fast away as do's the sunne:
And as a vapour, or a drop of raine
Once lost, can ne'r be found againe:

So when or you or I are made
A fable, song, or fleeting shade ;
All love, all liking, all delight
Lies drown'd with us in endlesse night.
Then while time serves, and we are but
    decaying ;
Come, my Corinna, come, let's goe a Maying.

—⋀⋁⋀⋁⋀—

To the Maids to Walke Abroad.

"Draw-gloves" (l. 5), a game with the fingers and bits of paper. Hesperides.

COME sit we under yonder tree,
Where merry as the maids we'l be.
And as on primroses we sit,
We'l venter (if we can) at wit :
If not, at draw-gloves we will play ;
So spend some minutes of the day :
Or else spin out the thread of sands,
Playing at questions and commands :
Or tell what strange tricks Love can do,
By quickly making one of two.
Thus we will sit and talke ; but tell
No cruell truths of Philomell,
Or Phillis, whom hard Fate forc't on,
To kill her selfe for Demophon.
But fables we'l relate ; how Jove
Put on all shapes to get a love :
As now a satyr, then a swan ;
A bull but then ; and now a man.

68

Herrick.

Next we will act, how young men wooe ;
And sigh, and kiss, as lovers do :
And talke of brides ; and who shall make
That wedding-smock, this bridal-cake ;
That dress, this sprig, that leaf, this vine ;
That smooth and silken Columbine.
This done, we'l draw lots, who shall buy
And guild the baies and rosemary :
What posies for our wedding rings ;
What gloves we'l give, and ribanings : .
And smiling at our selves, decree,
Who then the joyning priest shall be.
What short sweet prayers shall be said ;
And how the posset shall be made
With cream of lillies (not of kine)
And maiden's-blush, for spiced wine.
Thus, having talkt, we'l next commend
A kiss to each ; and so we'l end.

—◦◦◦◦◦—

The Bell-man. Hesperides.

FROM noise of scare-fires rest ye free,
From murders benedicitie.
From all mischances, that may fright
Your pleasing slumbers in the night :
Mercie secure ye all, and keep
The goblin from ye, while ye sleep.
Past one aclock, and almost two,
My masters all, *Good day to you.*

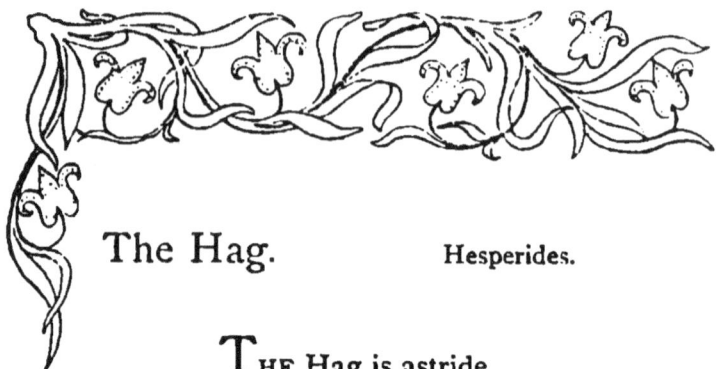

The Hag.

THE Hag is astride,
This night for to ride ;
The Devill and shee together :
Through thick, and through thin,
Now out, and then in,
Though ne'r so foule be the weather.

A thorn or a burr
She takes for a spurre :
With a lash of a bramble she rides now,
Through brakes and through bryars,
O're ditches, and mires,
She followes the spirit that guides now.

No beast, for his food,
Dares now range the wood ;
But husht in his laire he lies lurking :
While mischeifs, by these,
On land and on seas,
At noone of night are a working,

The storme will arise,
And trouble the skies ;
This night, and more for the wonder,
The ghost from the tomb
Affrighted shall come,
Cal'd out by the clap of the thunder.

The Old Wives Prayer.

Hesperides.

Holy-rood come forth and shield
Us i'th' citie, and the field :
Safely guard us, now and aye,
From the blast that burns by day ;
And those sounds that us affright
In the dead of dampish night.
Drive all hurtfull feinds us fro,
By the time the cocks first crow.

—∿∿∿—

The Fairies.

Hesperides.

If ye will with Mab find grace,
Set each platter in his place :
Rake the fier up, and get
Water in, ere sun be set.
Wash your pailes, and clense your dairies;
Sluts are loathsome to the fairies :
Sweep your house : who doth not so,
Mab will pinch her by the toe.

—∿∿∿—

Upon Mistresse Susanna South- well her Cheeks. Hesperides.

Rare are thy cheeks, Susanna, which do
show
Ripe cherries smiling, while that others blow.

—◁◁◁◁◁◁—

To·Musick.   "A Song." Hesper-
ides.

Musick, thou Queen of Heaven, care-
charming spel,
That strik'st a stilnesse into hell :
Thou that tam'st tygers, and fierce storms, that
rise,
        With thy soule-melting lullabies :
Fall down, down, down, from those thy
chiming spheres,
To charme our soules, as thou enchant'st our
eares.

—◁◁◁◁◁◁—

Herrick.

Lyrick for Legacies.

Hesperides.

Gold I've none, for use or show,
Neither silver to bestow
At my death ; but thus much know,
That each lyrick here shall be
Of my love a legacie,
Left to all posterity.
Gentle friends, then doe but please,
To accept such coynes as these ;
As my last remembrances.

—◇◇◇—

Upon the Losse of his Mistresses.

Hesperides.

I have lost, and lately, these
Many dainty mistresses :
Stately Julia, prime of all ;
Sapho next, a principall :
Smooth Anthea, for a skin
White, and heaven-like chrystalline :
Sweet Electra, and the choice
Myrha, for the lute, and voice.
Next, Corinna, for her wit,
And the graceful use of it :
With Perilla : all are gone ;
Onely Herrick's left alone,
For to number sorrow by
Their departures hence, and die.

73

The Departure of the Good Dæmon.

WHAT can I do in poetry,
Now the good spirit's gone from me?
Why nothing now, but lonely sit,
And over-read what I have writ.

—•ΛΛ\Λ—

Upon his Departure Hence.

THUS I
Passe by,
And die :
As one,
Unknown,
And gon :
I'm made
A shade,
And laid
I'th grave,
There have
My cave.
Where tell
I dwell,
Farewell.

74

To his Paternall Countrey.

Hesperides.

O EARTH ! earth ! earth ! heare thou my
  voice, and be
Loving, and gentle for to cover me :
Banish'd from thee I live ; ne'r to return,
Unlesse thou giv'st my small remains an urne.

—ᴡᴡᴡ—

To the Nightin-gale :

"And Robin Red-brest." Hesperides.

Wʜᴇɴ I departed am, ring thou my knell,
Thou pittifull, and pretty Philomel :
And when I'm laid out for a corse ; then be
Thou sexton, red-brest, for to cover me.

—ᴡᴡᴡ—

To the Yew and Cypresse :

"To grace his Funerall." Hesperides.

Bᴏᴛʜ you two have
  Relation to the grave :
  And where
The fun'rall-trump sounds, you are there.

Lyric Poems.

I shall be made
Ere long a fleeting shade :
Pray come,
And doe some honour to my tomb.

Do not deny
My last request ; for I
Will be
Thankfull to you, or friends, for me.

—⋀⋁⋀⋁—

No Shipwrack of Vertue.

"To a Friend." Hesperides.

THOU sail'st with others in this Argus here ;
Nor wrack or bulging thou hast cause to feare :
But trust to this, my noble passenger ;
Who swims with vertue, he shall still be sure
Ulysses-like, all tempests to endure ;
And 'midst a thousand gulfs to be secure.

—⋀⋁⋀⋁—

His Cavalier.

Hesperides.

GIVE me that man, that dares bestride
The active sea-horse, and with pride,
Through that huge field of waters ride :
Who, with his looks too, can appease
The ruffling winds and raging seas,
In mid'st of all their outrages.

76

Herrick.

This, this a virtuous man can doe,
Saile against rocks, and split them too ;
I ! and a world of pikes passe through.

—◇◇◇—

To the Lady Crew, upon the Death of her Child.

WHY, madam, will ye longer weep,
When as your baby's lull'd asleep?
And, pretty child, feeles now no more
Those paines it lately felt before.
All now is silent ; groanes are fled :
Your child lyes still, yet is not dead :
But rather like a flower hid here
To spring againe another yeare.

—◇◇◇—

Upon a Maide.   Hesperides

I.

HERE she lyes, in bed of spice,
Faire as Eve in paradice :
For her beauty it was such
Poets co'd not praise too much.

Virgins, come, and in a ring
Her supreamest requiem sing ;
Then depart, but see ye tread
Lightly, lightly ore the dead.

II.

GONE she is a long, long way,
But she has decreed a day
Back to come, and make no stay :
So we keepe, till her returne
Here, her ashes, or her urne.

—⋙—

An Epitaph
upon a Virgin.

Hesperides.

HERE a solemne fast we keepe,
While all beauty lyes asleep,
Husht be all things ; no noyse here,
But the toning of a teare :
Or a sigh of such as bring
Cowslips for her covering.

—⋙—

Upon a Child that Dyed.

I.

Here she lies, a pretty bud,
Lately made of flesh and blood :
Who, as soone, fell fast asleep,
As her little eyes did peep.
Give her strewings ; but not stir
The earth, that lightly covers her.

II.

Here a pretty baby lies
Sung asleep with lullabies :
Pray be silent, and not stirre
Th' easie earth that covers her.

—ᴧᴧᴧ—

To his dying Brother, Master William Herrick.

Life of my life, take not so soone thy flight,
But stay the time till we have bade Good night.
Thou hast both wind and tide with thee ; thy
    way
As soone dispatcht is by the night, as day.

Let us not then so rudely henceforth goe
Till we have wept, kist, sigh't, shook hands,
or so.
There's paine in parting ; and a kind of hell,
When once true-lovers take their last fare-well.
What? shall we two our endlesse leaves take
here
Without a sad looke, or a solemne teare?
He knowes not love, that hath not this truth
proved,
Love is most loth to leave the thing beloved.
Pay we our vowes, and goe ; yet when we part,
Then, even then, I will bequeath my heart
Into thy loving hands : for Ile keep none
To warme my breast, when thou my pulse art
gone.
No, here Ile last, and walk, a harmless shade,
About this urne, wherein thy dust is laid,
To guard it so, as nothing here shall be
Heavy, to hurt those sacred seeds of thee.

—◁◁◁—

An Ode to Master Endymion Porter :

"Upon his Brother's Death." Hesperides.

NOT all thy flushing sunnes are set,
Herrick, as yet :
Nor doth this far-drawn hemisphere
Frown, and look sullen ev'ry where.

Herrick.

Daies may conclude in nights ; and suns may
  rest,
    As dead, within the west ;
Yet the next morne, re-guild the fragrant east.

    Alas for me ! that I have lost
      E'en all almost :
    Sunk is my sight ; set is my sun ;
    And all the loome of life undone :
The staffe, the elme, the prop, the shelt'ring
  wall,
    Whereon my vine did crawle,
Now, now, blowne downe ; needs must the old
  stock fall.

    Yet, Porter, while thou keep'st alive,
      In death I thrive :
    And like a Phenix re-aspire
    From out my narde, and fun'rall fire :
    And as I prune my feather'd youth, so I
      Doe mar'l how I co'd die,
When I had thee, my chiefe preserver, by.

    I'm up, I'm up, and blesse that hand,
      Which makes me stand
    Now as I doe ; and but for thee,
    I must confesse, I co'd not be.
The debt is paid : for he who doth resigne
      Thanks to the gen'rous vine ;
Invites fresh grapes to fill his presse with wine.

Upon Himselfe.

I co'd never love indeed ;
Never see mine own heart bleed :
Never crucifie my life ;
Or for widow, maid, or wife.

I co'd never seeke to please
One, or many mistresses :
Never like their lips, to sweare
Oyle of roses still smelt there.

I co'd never breake my sleepe,
Fold mine armes, sob, sigh, or weep :
Never beg, or humbly wooe
With oathes, and lyes, as others do.

I co'd never walke alone ;
Put a shirt of sackcloth on :
Never keep a fast, or pray
For good luck in love (that day).

But have hitherto liv'd free,
As the aire that circles me :
And kept credit with my heart,
Neither broke i'th whole, or part.

—◡◡◡—

A Nuptiall Song :

" Or Epithalamie, on Sir Clipseby Crew and his Lady." Hesperides.

WHAT'S that we see from far? the spring of
day
Bloom'd from the east, or faire injewel'd May
Blowne out of April; or some new-
Star fill'd with glory to our view.
Reaching at heaven,
To adde a nobler planet to the seven?
Say, or doe we not descrie
Some goddesse, in a cloud of tiffanie
To move, or rather the
Emergent Venus from the sea?

'Tis she ! 'tis she ! or else some more divine
Enlightned substance; mark how from the
shrine
Of holy saints she paces on,
Treading upon vermilion
And amber; spice-
ing the chafte aire with fumes of paradise.
Then come on, come on, and yeeld
A savour like unto a blessed field,
When the bedabled morne
Washes the golden eares of corne.

Lyric Poems.

See where she comes ; and smell how all the
    street
Breathes vine-yards and pomgranats ; O how
    sweet !
    As a fir'd altar, is each stone,
    Perspiring pounded cynamon.
            The phenix nest,
Built up of odours, burneth in her breast.
    Who therein wo'd not consume
    His soule to ash-heaps in that rich perfume ?
            Bestroaking Fate the while
    He burnes to embers on the pile.

Himen, O Himen ! tread the sacred ground ;
Shew thy white feet, and head with marjoram
    crown'd :
    Mount up thy flames, and let thy torch
    Display the bridegroom in the porch,
            In his desires
More towring, more disparkling then thy fires ;
    Shew her how his eyes do turne
And roule about, and in their motions burne
            Their balls to cindars : haste,
    Or else to ashes he will waste.

Glide by the banks of virgins then, and passe
The shewers of roses, lucky foure-leav'd grasse :
    The while the cloud of younglings sing,
    And drown yee with a flowrie spring :
            While some repeat
Your praise, and bless you, sprinkling you with
    wheat :

Herrick.

While that others doe divine ;
Blest is the bride, on whom the sun doth shine ;
    And thousands gladly wish
    You multiply, as doth a fish.

And beautious bride we do confess y'are wise,
In dealing forth these bashfull jealousies ;
    In Love's name do so ; and a price
    Set on your selfe, by being nice :
        But yet take heed ;
What now you seem, be not the same indeed,
    And turne apostate : Love will
Part of the way be met ; or sit stone-still.
        On then, and though you slow-
    ly go, yet, howsoever, go.

And now y'are enter'd ; see the codled cook
Runs from his torrid zone, to prie, and look,
    And blesse his dainty mistresse : see,
    The aged point out, This is she,
        Who now must sway
The house (Love shield her) with her yea and
    nay :
    And the smirk butler thinks it
Sin, in's nap'rie, not to express his wit ;
        Each striving to devise
    Some gin, wherewith to catch your eyes.

To bed, to bed, kind turtles, now, and write
This the short'st day, and this the longest
    night ;
    But yet too short for you : 'tis we,
    Who count this night as long as three,
        Lying alone,
Telling the clock strike ten, eleven, twelve, one.

Lyric Poems.

Quickly, quickly then prepare ;
And let the young-men and the bride-maids share
         Your garters ; and their joynts
Encircle with the bride-grooms points.

By the bride's eyes, and by the teeming life
Of her green hopes, we charge ye, that no
         strife,
Farther then gentleness tends, gets place
Among ye, striving for her lace :
         O doe not fall
Foule in these noble pastimes, lest ye call
         Discord in, and so divide
The youthfull bride-groom, and the fragrant
         bride :
         Which Love forefend ; but spoken,
Be't to your praise, no peace was broken.

Strip her of spring-time, tender whimpring
         maids,
Now autumne's come, when all those flowrie
         aids
Of her delayes must end ; dispose
That lady-smock, that pansie, and that
         rose
         Neatly apart ;
But for prick-madam, and for gentle-heart ;
And soft maidens-blush, the bride
Makes holy these, all others lay aside :
         Then strip her, or unto her
Let him come, who dares undo her.

And to enchant yee more, see every where
About the roofe a syren in a sphere,

Herrick.

As we think, singing to the dinne
Of many a warbling cherubim :
       O marke yee how
The soule of nature melts in numbers : now
    See, a thousand Cupids flye,
To light their tapers at the bride's bright eye.
       To bed ; or her they'l tire,
    Were she an element of fire.

And to your more bewitching, see, the proud
Plumpe bed beare up, and swelling like a cloud,
    Tempting the two too modest ; can
    Yee see it brusle like a swan,
       And you be cold
To meet it, when it woo's and seemes to fold
    The armes to hugge it ? throw, throw
Your selves into the mighty over-flow
       Of that white pride, and drowne
    The night, with you, in floods of downe.

The bed is ready, and the maze of love
Lookes for the treaders ; every where is wove
    Wit and new misterie ; read, and
    Put in practise, to understand
       And know each wile,
Each hieroglyphick of a kisse or smile ;
    And do it to the full ; reach
High in your own conceipt, and some wa
    teach
       Nature and art, one more
    Play, then they ever knew before.

If needs we must for ceremonies-sake,
Blesse a sack-posset ; luck go with it ; take

Lyric Poems.

The night-charme quickly; you have spells,
And magicks for to end, and hells,
   To passe ; but such
And of such torture as no one would grutch
  To live therein for ever : frie
And consume, and grow again to die,
      And live, and in that case
  Love the confusion of the place.

But since it must be done, dispatch, and sowe
Up in a sheet your bride, and what if so
  It be with rock, or walles of brasse,
  Ye towre her up, as Danae was ;
      Thinke you that this,
Or hell it selfe a powerfull bulwarke is ?
  I tell yee no ; but like a
Bold bolt of thunder he will make his way,
      And rend the cloud, and throw
The sheet about, like flakes of snow.

All now is husht in silence ; midwife-moone,
With all her owle-ey'd issue, begs a boon
  Which you must grant ; that's entrance ;
  with
  Which extract, all we can call pith
      And quintiscence
Of planetary bodies ; so commence
  All faire constellations
Looking upon yee, that, that nations
      Springing from two such fires
May blaze the vertue of their sires.

The Poet's Good Wishes:

" For the most hope-full and handsome Prince, the Duke of Yorke."
Hesperides.

May his pretty duke-ship grow
Like t'a rose of Jericho :
Sweeter far, then ever yet
Showrs or sun-shines co'd beget.
May the graces, and the howers
Strew his hopes, and him with flowers :
And so dresse him up with love,
As to be the chick of Jove.
May the thrice-three-sisters sing
Him the soveraigne of their spring :
And entitle none to be
Prince of Hellicon, but he.
May his soft foot, where it treads,
Gardens thence produce and meads :
And those meddowes full be set
With the rose, and violet
May his ample name be knowne
To the last succession :
And his actions high be told
Through the world, but writ in gold.

The Meddow Verse.

"Or Aniversary to Mistris Bridget Low-man." Hesperides.

I.

COME with the spring-time forth, fair maid,
and be
This year again, the medow's deity.
Yet ere ye enter, give us leave to set
Upon your head this flowry coronet :
To make this neat distinction from the rest ;
You are the prime, and princesse of the feast :
To which, with silver feet lead you the way,
While sweet-breath nimphs, attend on you this
day.
This is your houre ; and best you may com-
mand,
Since you are lady of this fairie land.
Full mirth wait on you ; and such mirth as
shall
Cherrish the cheek, but make none blush at all.

II.

THE PARTING VERSE, THE FEAST THERE ENDED.

LOTH to depart, but yet at last, each one
Back must now go to's habitation :
Not knowing thus much, when we once do
sever,
Whether or no, that we shall meet here ever.
As for my self, since time a thousand cares
And griefs hath fil'de upon my silver hairs ;

'Tis to be doubted whether I next yeer,
Or no, shall give ye a re-meeting here.
If die I must, then my last vow shall be,
You'l with a tear or two, remember me,
Your sometime poet ; but if fates do give
Me longer date, and more fresh springs to live :
Oft as your field, shall her old age renew,
Herrick shall make the meddow-verse for you.

To Groves. Hesperides.

YEE silent shades, whose each tree here
Some relique of a saint doth weare :
Who for some sweet-hearts sake, did prove
The fire, and martyrdome of love.
Here is the legend of those saints
That di'd for love ; and their complaints :
Their wounded hearts ; and names we find
Encarv'd upon the leaves and rind.
Give way, give way to me, who come
Scorch't with the selfe-same martyrdome :
And have deserv'd as much, Love knowes,
As to be canoniz'd 'mongst those,
Whose deeds, and deaths here written are
Within your greenie-kalendar :
By all those virgins fillets hung
Upon your boughs, and requiems sung
For saints and soules departed hence,
(Here honour'd still with frankincense)
By all those teares that have been shed,
As a drink-offering, to the dead :

Lyric Poems.

By all those true-love-knots, that be
With motto's carv'd on every tree,
By sweet S. Phillis ; pitie me :
By deare S. Iphis ; and the rest,
Of all those other saints now blest ;
Me, me, forsaken, here admit
Among your mirtles to be writ :
That my poore name may have the glory
To live remembred in your story.

—◦◦◦—

An Ode to
Sir Clipsebie   Hesperides.
Crew.

HERE we securely live, and eate
              The creame of meat ;
        And keep eternal fires,
By which we sit, and doe divine
              As wine
        And rage inspires.

If full we charme ; then call upon
              Anacreon
        To grace the frantick thyrse :
And having drunk, we raise a shout
              Throughout
        To praise his verse.

92

Herrick.

Then cause we Horace to be read,
        Which sung, or seyd,
    A goblet, to the brim,
Of lyrick wine, both swell'd and crown'd,
        A round
        We quaffe to him.

Thus, thus, we live, and spend the houres
        In wine and flowers :
    And make the frollick yeere,
The month, the week, the instant day
        To stay
        The longer here.

Come then, brave knight, and see the cell
        Wherein I dwell ;
    And my enchantments too ;
Which love and noble freedome is ;
        And this
        Shall fetter you.

Take horse, and come ; or be so kind,
        To send your mind
    (Though but in numbers few)
And I shall think I have the heart,
        Or part
        Of Clipseby Crew.

—◊◊◊—

A Country Life.

" To his brother, M. Tho: Herrick." Hesperides. " Brasse," money. " Tearcely," temperately.

THRICE, and above blest, my soules halfe, art
      thou,
    In thy both last, and better vow :
Could'st leave the city, for exchange, to see
    The countries sweet simplicity :
And it to know, and practice ; with intent
    To grow the sooner innocent :
By studying to know vertue ; and to aime
    More at her nature, then her name :
The last is but the least ; the first doth tell
    Wayes lesse to live, then to live well :
And both are knowne to thee, who now can'st
      live
    Led by thy conscience ; to give
Justice to soone-pleas'd nature ; and to show,
    Wisdome and she together goe,
And keep one centre : this with that conspires,
    To teach man to confine desires :
And know, that riches have their proper stint,
    In the contented mind, not mint.
And can'st instruct, that those who have the
      itch
    Of craving more, are never rich.
These things thou know'st to'th'height, and
      dost prevent
    That plague ; because thou art content

Herrick.

With that Heav'n gave thee with a warie hand,
    (More blessed in thy Brasse, then land)
To keep cheap nature even, and upright ;
    To coole, not cocker appetite.
Thus thou canst tearcely live to satisfie
    The belly chiefly ; not the eye :
Keeping the barking stomach wisely quiet,
    Lesse with a neat, then needfull diet.
But that which most makes sweet thy country
        life,
    Is, the fruition of a wife :
Whom, stars consenting with thy fate, thou
        hast
    Got, not so beautifull, as chast :
By whose warme side thou dost securely sleep,
    While Love the centinell doth keep,
With those deeds done by day, which n'er
        affright
    Thy silken slumbers in the night.
Nor has the darknesse power to usher in
    Feare to those sheets, that know no sin.
But still thy wife, by chast intentions led,
    Gives thee each night a maidenhead.
The damaskt medowes, and the peebly
        streames
    Sweeten, and make soft your dreames :
The purling springs, groves, birds, and well-
        weav'd bowrs,
    With fields enameled with flowers,
Present their shapes ; while fantasie discloses
    Millions of lillies mixt with roses.
Then dream, ye heare the lamb by many a
        bleat
    Woo'd to come suck the milkie teat ;

Lyric Poems

While Faunus in the vision comes to keep,
    From rav'ning wolves, the fleecie sheep.
With thousand such enchanting dreams, that
    meet
To make sleep not so sound, as sweet :
    Nor can these figures so thy rest endeare,
    As not to rise when Chanticlere
Warnes the last watch ; but with the dawne
    dost rise
    To work, but first to sacrifice ;
Making thy peace with heav'n, for some late
    fault,
    With holy-meale, and spirting-salt.
Which done, thy painfull thumb this sentence
    tells us,
    Jove for our labour all things sells us.
Nor are thy daily and devout affaires
    Attended with those desp'rate cares,
Th' industrious merchant has ; who for to find
    Gold, runneth to the Western Inde,
And back again ; tortur'd with fears, doth fly,
    Untaught, to suffer poverty.
But thou at home, blest with securest ease,
    Sitt'st, and beleev'st that there be seas,
And watrie dangers ; while thy whiter hap,
    But sees these things within thy map.
And viewing them with a more safe survey,
    Mak'st easie feare unto thee say,
A heart thrice wall'd with oke, and brasse, that
    man
    Had, first, durst plow the ocean.
But thou at home without or tyde or gale,
    Canst in thy map securely saile :
Seeing those painted countries ; and so guesse

Herrick.

By those fine shades, their substances :
And from thy compasse taking small advice,
    Buy'st travell at the lowest price.
Nor are thine eares so deafe, but thou canst
    heare,
    Far more with wonder, then with feare,
Fame tell of states, of countries, courts, and
    kings ;
    And beleeve there be such things :
When of these truths, thy happyer knowledge
    lyes,
    More in thine eares, then in thine eyes.
And when thou hear'st by that too-true-report,
    Vice rules the most, or all at court :
Thy pious wishes are, though thou not there,
    Vertue had, and mov'd her sphere.
But thou liv'st fearlesse ; and thy face ne'r
    shewes
    Fortune when she comes, or goes.
But with thy equall thoughts, prepar'd dost
    stand,
    To take her by the either hand :
Nor car'st which comes the first, the foule or
    faire ;
    A wise man ev'ry way lies square.
And like a surly oke, with storms perplext ;
    Growes still the stronger, strongly vext.
Be so, bold spirit ; stand center - like, un-
    mov'd ;
.   And be not onely thought, but prov'd
To be what I report thee ; and inure
    Thy selfe, if want comes to endure :
And so thou dost : for thy desires are
    Confin'd to live with private Larr :

Lyric Poems.

Not curious whether appetite be fed,
  Or with the first, or second bread.
Who keep'st no proud mouth for delicious cates :
  Hunger makes coorse meats, delicates.
Can'st, and unurg'd, forsake that larded fare,
  Which art, not nature, makes so rare ;
To taste boyl'd nettles, colworts, beets, and eate
  These, and sowre herbs, as dainty meat ?
While soft opinion makes thy Genius say,
  Content makes all ambrosia.
Nor is it, that thou keep'st this stricter size
  So much for want, as exercise :
To numb the sence of dearth, which sho'd
    sinne haste it,
  Thou might'st but onely see't, not taste it.
Yet can thy humble roofe maintaine a quire
  Of singing crickits by thy fire :
And the brisk mouse may feast her selfe with
    crums,
  Till that the green-ey'd kitling comes.
Then to her cabbin, blest she can escape
  The sudden danger of a rape.
And thus thy little-well-kept stock doth prove,
  Wealth cannot make a life, but Love.
Nor art thou so close-handed, but can'st spend
  (Counsell concurring with the end)
As well as spare : still conning o'r this theame,
  To shun the first, and last extreame.
Ordaining that thy small stock find no breach,
  Or to exceed thy tether's reach :
But to live round, and close, and wisely true
  To thine owne selfe ; and knowne to few.
Thus let thy rurall sanctuary be
  Elizium to thy wife and thee ;

Herrick.

There to disport your selves with golden
    measure :
    For seldome use commends the pleasure.
Live, and live blest ; thrice happy paire ; let
    breath,
    But lost to one, be th' others death.
And as there is one love, one faith, one troth,
    Be so one death, one grave to both.
Till when, in such assurance live, ye may
    Nor feare, or wish your dying day.

—◦◦◦◦—

His Content in the Country.

Hesperides.

HERE, here I live with what my board,
Can with the smallest cost afford.
Though ne'r so mean the viands be,
They well content my Prew and me.
Or pea, or bean, or wort, or beet,
What ever comes, content makes sweet :
Here we rejoyce, because no rent
We pay for our poore tenement :
Wherein we rest, and never feare
The landlord, or the usurer.
The quarter-day do's ne'r affright
Our peacefull slumbers in the night.
We eate our own, and batten more,
Because we feed on no mans score :
But pitie those, whose flanks grow great,
Swel'd with the lard of others meat.

99

We blesse our fortunes, when we see
Our own beloved privacie :
And like our living, where w'are known
To very few, or else to none.

—∿∿∿—

The Hock-cart, or Harvest Home.

"Maukin" (l. 9), baker's clout. "Fill-horse" (l. 21), shaft-horse." Hesperides.

Come, sons of summer, by whose toile,
We are the lords of wine and oile :
By whose tough labours, and rough hands,
We rip up first, then reap our lands.
Crown'd with the eares of corne, now come,
And, to the pipe, sing harvest home.
Come forth, my lord, and see the cart
Drest up with all the country art.
See, here a maukin, there a sheet,
As spotlesse pure, as it is sweet :
The horses, mares, and frisking fillies,
Clad, all, in linnen, white as lillies.
The harvest swaines, and wenches bound
For joy, to see the hock-cart crown'd.
About the cart, heare, how the rout
Of rurall younglings raise the shout ;
Pressing before, some coming after,
Those with a shout, and these with laughter.
Some blesse the cart ; some kisse the sheaves ;
Some prank them up with oaken leaves :
Some crosse the fill-horse ; some with great
Devotion, stroak the home-borne wheat :

Herrick.

While other rusticks, lesse attent
To prayers, then to merryment,
Run after with their breeches rent.
Well, on, brave boyes, to your lord's hearth,
Glitt'ring with fire ; where, for your mirth,
Ye shall see first the large and cheefe
Foundation of your feast, fat beefe :
With upper stories, mutton, veale
And bacon, which makes full the meale,
With sev'rall dishes standing by,
As here a custard, there a pie,
And here all tempting frumentie.
And for to make the merry cheere,
If smirking wine be wanting here,
There's that, which drowns all care, stout beere ;
Which freely drink to your lord's health,
Then to the plough, the common-wealth ;
Next to your flailes, your fanes, your fatts ;
Then to the maids with wheaten hats :
To the rough sickle, and crookt sythe,
Drink, frollick, boyes, till all be blythe.
Feed, and grow fat ; and as ye eat,
Be mindfull, that the lab'ring neat,
As you, may have their fill of meat.
And know, besides, ye must revoke
The patient oxe unto the yoke,
And all goe back unto the plough
And harrow, though they'r hang'd up now.
And, you must know, your lord's word's true,
Feed him ye must, whose food fils you.
And that this pleasure is like raine,
Not sent ye for to drowne your paine,
But for to make it spring againe.

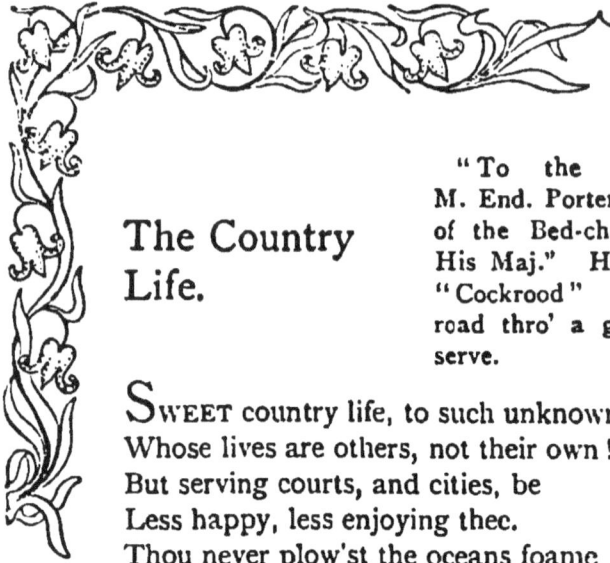

The Country Life.

" To the honoured M. End. Porter, Groome of the Bed-chamber to His Maj." Hesperides. "Cockrood" (p. 104), road thro' a game pre-serve.

Sweet country life, to such unknown,
Whose lives are others, not their own !
But serving courts, and cities, be
Less happy, less enjoying thee.
Thou never plow'st the oceans foame
To seeke, and bring rough pepper home :
Nor to the Eastern Ind dost rove
To bring from thence the scorched clove.
Nor, with the losse of thy lov'd rest,
Bring'st home the ingot from the West.
No, thy ambition's master-piece
Flies no thought higher then a fleece :
Or how to pay thy hinds, and cleere
All scores ; and so to end the yeere :
But walk'st about thine own dear bounds,
Not envying others larger grounds :
For well thou know'st, *'tis not th' extent
Of land makes life, but sweet content.*
When now the cock (the plow-mans horne)
Calls forth the lilly-wristed morne ;
Then to thy corn-fields thou dost goe,
Which though well soyl'd, yet thou dost know,
That the best compost for the lands
Is the wise masters feet, and hands.

Herrick.

There at the plough thou find'st thy teame
With a hind whistling there to them :
And cheer'st them up, by singing how
The kingdoms portion is the plow.
This done, then to th' enameld meads
Thou go'st ; and as thy foot there treads,
Thou seest a present God-like power
Imprinted in each herbe and flower :
And smell'st the breath of great-ey'd kine,
Sweet as the blossomes of the vine.
Here thou behold'st thy large sleek neat
Unto the dew-laps up in meat :
And, as thou look'st, the wanton steere,
The heifer, cow, and oxe draw neere
To make a pleasing pastime there.
These seen, thou go'st to view thy flocks
Of sheep, safe from the wolfe and fox,
And find'st their bellies there as full
Of short sweet grasse, as backs with wool.
And leav'st them, as they feed and fill,
A shepherd piping on a hill.
For sports, for pagentrie, and playes,
Thou hast thy eves, and holydayes ;
On which the young men and maids meet,
To exercise their dancing feet :
Tripping the comely country round,
With daffadils and daisies crown'd.
Thy wakes, thy quintels, here thou hast,
Thy May-poles too with garlands grac't :
Thy Morris-dance ; thy Whitsun-ale ;
Thy sheering-feast, which never faile.
Thy harvest home ; thy wassaile bowle,
That's tost up after Fox i'th' hole.
Thy mummeries ; thy Twelfe-tide kings

Lyric Poems.

And queenes ; thy Christmas revellings :
Thy nut-browne mirth ; thy russet wit ;
And no man payes too deare for it.
To these, thou hast thy times to goe
And trace the hare i'th' trecherous snow :
Thy witty wiles to draw, and get
The larke into the trammell net :
Thou hast thy cockrood, and thy glade
To take the precious phesant made :
Thy lime-twigs, snares, and pit-falls then
To catch the pilfring birds, not men.
O happy life ! if that their good
The husbandmen but understood !
Who all the day themselves doe please,
And younglings, with such sports as these.
And, lying down, have nought t' affright
Sweet sleep, that makes more short the night.
Cætera desunt——

—ᴡᴡᴡ—

His Fare-well
to Sack.

[1629]. Hesperides.

Farewell, thou thing, time-past so knowne,
  so deare
To me, as blood to life and spirit : neare,
Nay, thou more neare then kindred, friend,
  man, wife,
Male to the female, soule to body : life
To quick action, or the warme soft side
Of the resigning, yet resisting bride.

104

Herrick.

The kisse of virgins ; first-fruits of the bed ;
Soft speech, smooth touch, the lips, the
    maidenhead :
These, and a thousand sweets, co'd never be
So neare, or deare, as thou wast once to me.
O thou the drink of gods, and angels ! wine
That scatter'st spirit and lust ; whose purest
    shine,
More radiant then the summers sun-beams
    shows ;
Each way illustrious, brave ; and like to those
Comets we see by night ; whose shagg'd por-
    tents
Fore-tell the comming of some dire events :
Or some full flame, which with a pride aspires,
Throwing about his wild, and active fires.
'Tis thou, above nectar, O divinest soule !
(Eternall in thy self) that canst controule
That, which subverts whole nature, grief and
    care ;
Vexation of the mind, and damn'd despaire.
'Tis thou, alone, who with thy mistick fan,
Work'st more then wisdome, art, or nature can,
To rouze the sacred madnesse ; and awake
The frost-bound-blood, and spirits ; and to
    make
Them frantick with thy raptures, flashing
    through
The soule, like lightning, and as active too.
'Tis not Apollo can, or those thrice three
Castalian sisters, sing, if wanting thee.
Horace, Anacreon both had lost their fame,
Hadst thou not fill'd them with thy fire and
    flame.

Lyric Poems.

Phæbean splendour! and thou Thespian spring!
Of which, sweet swans must drink, before they
    sing
Their true-pac'd numbers, and their holy-layes,
Which makes them worthy cedar, and the
    bayes.
But why? why longer doe I gaze upon
Thee with the eye of admiration?
Since I must leave thee; and enforc'd, must
    say
To all thy witching beauties, Goe, away.
But if thy whimpring looks doe ask me why?
Then know, that nature bids thee goe, not I.
'Tis her erroneous self has made a braine
Uncapable of such a soveraigne,
As is thy powerfull selfe.   Prethee not smile;
Or smile more inly; lest thy looks beguile
My vowes denounc'd in zeale, which thus much
    show thee,
That I have sworn, but by thy looks to know
    thee.
Let others drink thee freely; and desire
Thee and their lips espous'd; while I admire,
And love thee; but not taste thee.   Let my
    muse
Faile of thy former helps; and onely use
Her inadult'rate strength: what's done by me
Hereafter, shall smell of the lamp, not thee.

—\/\/\/\—

Herrick.

A Pastorall.

"Sung to the King."
Montano, Silvio, and
Mirtillo, Shepheards.
Hesperides.

Mon. BAD are the times.   *Sil.* And wors
   then they are we.
Mon. Troth, bad are both ; worse fruit, and
   ill the tree :
The feast arc shepheards fail.   *Sil.* None
   crowns the cup
Of wassaile now, or sets the quintell up :
And he, who us'd to leade the country-round,
Youthfull Mirtillo, here he comes, grief drownd.
   Ambo. Lets cheer him up.   *Sil.* Behold him
   weeping ripe.
Mir. Ah ! Amarillis, farewell mirth and pipe ;
Since thou art gone, no more I mean to play,
To these smooth lawns, my mirthfull roundelay.
Dear Amarillis !   *Mon.* Hark !   *Sil.* mark :
   Mir. this earth grew sweet
Where, Amarillis, thou didst set thy feet.
   Ambo. Poor pittied youth !   *Mir.* And here
   the breth of kine
And sheep, grew more sweet, by that breth of
   thine.
This flock of wooll, and this rich lock of hair,
This ball of cow-slips, these she gave me here.
   Sil. Words sweet as love it self.   Montano,
   hark.
Mir. This way she came, and this way too
   she went ;
How each thing smells divinely redolent !

107

Lyric Poems.

Like to a field of beans, when newly blown ;
Or like a medow being lately mown.
Mon. A sweet-sad passion.——
Mir. In dewie-mornings when she came
    this way,
Sweet bents wode bow, to give my love the day :
And when at night, she folded had her sheep,
Daysies wo'd shut, and closing, sigh and weep.
Besides, ai me ! since she went hence to dwell,
The voices daughter nea'r spake syllable.
But she is gone. *Sil.* Mirtillo, tell us whether,
    Mir. Where she and I shall never meet
    together.
    Mon. Fore-fend it Pan, and Pales do thou
    please
To give an end : *Mir.* To what ? *Sil.* such
    griefs as these.
Mir. Never, O never ! Still I may endure
The wound I suffer, never find a cure.
    Mont. Love for thy sake will bring her to
    these hills
And dales again : *Mir.* No I will languish
    still ;
And all the while my part shall be to weepe ;
And with my sighs, call home my bleating
    sheep :
And in the rind of every comely tree
Ile carve thy name, and in that name kisse
    thee :
    Mon. Set with the sunne, thy woes : *Sil.* The
    day grows old :
And time it is our full-fed flocks to fold.
    Chor. The shades grow great ; but greater
    growes our sorrow,

But lets go steepe
Our eyes in sleepe ;
And meet to weepe
        To morrow.

—⋀⋁⋀⋁⋀—

A Paranæticall,
or Advisive
Verse, to his   Hesperides.
Friend, M.
John Wicks.

Is this a life, to break thy sleep?
To rise as soon as day doth peep?
To tire thy patient oxe or asse
By noone, and let thy good dayes passe,
Not knowing this, that Jove decrees
Some mirth, t'adulce mans miseries?
No ; 'tis a life, to have thine oyle,
Without extortion, from thy soyle :
Thy faithfull fields to yeeld thee graine,
Although with some, yet little paine :
To have thy mind, and nuptiall bed,
With feares, and cares uncumbered :
A pleasing wife, that by thy side
Lies softly panting like a bride.
This is to live, and to endeere
Those minutes, Time has lent us here.
Then, while Fates suffer, live thou free,
As is that ayre that circles thee,

And crown thy temples too, and let
Thy servant, not thy own self, sweat,
To strut thy barnes with sheafs of wheat.
Time steals away like to a stream,
And we glide hence away with them.
No sound recalls the houres once fled,
Or roses, being withered:
Nor us, my friend, when we are lost,
Like to a deaw, or melted frost.
Then live we mirthfull, while we should,
And turn the iron age to gold.
Let's feast, and frolick, sing, and play,
And thus lesse last, then live our day.
Whose life with care is overcast,
That man's not said to live, but last:
Nor is't a life, seven yeares to tell,
But for to live that half seven well:
And that wee'l do; as men, who know,
Some few sands spent, we hence must go,
Both to be blended in the urn,
From whence there's never a return.

—◇◇◇◇—

To the Little Spinners.

(" Spinner " was an old name for Spider.) Hesperides.

Y EE pretty huswives, wo'd ye know
The worke that I wo'd put ye to?
This, this it sho'd be, for to spin,
A lawn for me, so fine and thin,
As it might serve me for my skin.

Herrick.

For cruell Love ha's me so whipt,
That of my skin, I all am stript;
And shall dispaire, that any art
Can ease the rawnesse, or the smart;
Unlesse you skin again each part.
Which mercy if you will but do
I call all maids to witnesse too
What here I promise, that no broom
Shall now, or ever after come
To wrong a spinner or her loome.

The Fairie Temple:

"Or, Oberon's Chappell." Dedicated to Mr John Merrifield, Counsellor at Law. Hesperides. "Bruckelled" (l. 64), wet and dirty.

RARE temples thou hast seen, I know,
And rich for in and outward show :
Survey this chappell, built, alone,
Without or lime, or wood, or stone :
Then say, if one th'ast seene more fine
Then this, the fairies once, now thine.

The Temple.

A way enchac't with glasse and beads
There is, that to the chappel leads :
Whose structure, for his holy rest,
Is here the halcion's curious nest :
Into the which who looks shall see
His temple of idolatry :
Where he of god-heads has such store,
As Rome's Pantheon had not more.
His house of Rimmon, this he calls,
Girt with small bones, instead of walls.
First, in a neech, more black then jet,
His idol-cricket there is set :
Then in a polisht ovall by
There stands his idol-beetle-flie :
Next in an arch, akin to this,
His idol-canker seated is :

Herrick.

Then in a round, is plac't by these,
His golden god, Cantharides.
So that where ere ye look, ye see,
No capitoll, no cornish free,
Or freeze, from this fine fripperie.
Now this the fairies wo'd have known,
Theirs is a mixt religion.
And some have heard the elves it call
Part pagan, part papisticall.
If unto me all tongues were granted,
I co'd not speak the saints here painted.
Saint Tit, Saint Nit, Saint Is, Saint Itis,
Who 'gainst Mabs state plac't here right is.
Saint Will o'th'wispe, of no great bignes,
But alias call'd here *fatuus ignis*.
Saint Frip, Saint Trip, Saint Fill, S. Fillie,
Neither those other-saint-ships will I
Here goe about for to recite
Their number, almost infinite,
Which one by one here set downe are
In this most curious calendar.
First, at the entrance of the gate,
A little-puppet-priest doth wait,
Who squeaks to all the commers there,
Favour your tongues, who enter here.
Pure hands bring hither, without staine.
A second pules, *Hence, hence, profane.*
Hard by, i'th'shell of halfe a nut,
The holy-water there is put :
A little brush of squirrils haires,
Compos'd of odde, not even paires,
Stands in the platter, or close by,
To purge the fairie family.
Neere to the altar stands the priest,

Lyric Poems.

There off'ring up the holy-grist :
Ducking in mood, and perfect tense,
With (much-good-do't him) reverence.
The altar is not here foure-square,
Nor in a forme triangular ;
Nor made of glasse, or wood, or stone,
But of a little transverce bone ;
Which boyes, and bruckel'd children call
(Playing for points and pins) cockall.
Whose linnen-drapery is a thin
Subtile and ductile codlin's skin ;
Which o're the board is smoothly spred,
With little seale-work damasked.
The fringe that circumbinds it too,
Is spangle-work of trembling dew,
Which, gently gleaming, makes a show,
Like frost-work glitt'ring on the snow.
Upon this fetuous board doth stand
Something for shew-bread, and at hand
(Just in the middle of the altar)
Upon an end, the fairie-psalter,
Grac't with the trout-flies curious wings,
Which serve for watched ribbanings.
Now, we must know, the elves are led
Right by the rubrick, which they read.
And if report of them be true,
They have their text for what they doe ;
I, and their book of Canons too.
And, as Sir Thomas Parson tells,
They have their book of Articles :
And if that fairie knight not lies,
They have their book of Homilies :
And other Scriptures, that designe
A short, but righteous discipline.

Herrick.

The bason stands the board upon
To take the free-oblation :
A little pin-dust ; which they hold
More precious, then we prize our gold :
Which charity they give to many
Poore of the parish, if there's any.
Upon the ends of these neat railes
Hatcht, with the silver-light of snails,
The elves, in formall manner, fix
Two pure, and holy candlesticks :
In either which a small tall bent
Burns for the altar's ornament.
For sanctity, they have, to these
Their curious copes and surplices
Of cleanest cobweb, hanging by
In their religious vesterie.
They have their ash-pans, and their brooms
To purge the chappel and the rooms :
Their many mumbling masse-priests here,
And many a dapper chorister.
There ush'ring vergers, here likewise,
Their canons, and their chaunteries :
Of cloyster-monks they have enow,
I, and their abby-lubbers too :
And if their legend doe not lye,
They much affect the papacie :
And since the last is dead, there's hope,
Elve Boniface shall next be pope.
They have their cups and chalices ;
Their pardons and indulgencies :
Their beads of nits, bels, books, and wax
Candles, forsooth, and other knacks :
Their holy oyle, their fasting-spittle ;
Their sacred salt here, not a little.

Lyric Poems.

Dry chips, old shooes, rags, grease, and bones ;
Beside their fumigations,
To drive the devill from the cod-piece
Of the fryar, of work an odde-piece.
Many a trifle too, and trinket,
And for what use, scarce man wo'd think it.
Next, then, upon the chanters side
An apples-core is hung up dry'd,
With ratling kirnils, which is rung
To call to morn, and even-song.
The saint, to which the most he prayes
And offers incense nights and dayes,
The lady of the lobster is,
Whose foot-pace he doth stroak and kisse ;
And, humbly, chives of saffron brings,
For his most cheerfull offerings.
When, after these, h'as paid his vows,
He lowly to the altar bows :
And then he dons the silk-worms shed,
Like a Turks turbant on his head,
And reverently departeth thence,
Hid in a cloud of frankincense :
And by the glow-worms light wel guided,
Goes to the feast that's now provided.

—〜〜〜—

Oberon's Feast.

SHAPCOT! to thee the fairy state
I, with discretion, dedicate.
Because thou prizest things that are
Curious, and un-familiar.
Take first the feast ; these dishes gone ;
Wee'll see the fairy-court anon.

A LITTLE mushroome table spred,
After short prayers, they set on bread ;
A moon-parcht grain of purest wheat,
With some small glit'ring gritt, to eate
His choyce bitts with ; then in a trice
They make a feast lesse great then nice.
But all this while his eye is serv'd,
We must not thinke his eare was sterv'd :
But that there was in place to stir
His spleen, the chirring grashopper ;
The merry cricket, puling flie,
The piping gnat for minstralcy.
And now, we must imagine first,
The elves present to quench his thirst
A pure seed-pearle of infant dew,
Brought and besweetned in a blew
And pregnant violet ; which done,
His kitling eyes begin to runne
Quite through the table, where he spies
The hornes of paperie butterflies,
Of which he eates, and tastes a little
Of that we call the cuckoes spittle.

Lyric Poems.

A little fuz-ball pudding stands
By, yet not blessed by his hands,
That was too coorse ; but then forthwith
He ventures boldly on the pith
Of sugred rush, and eates the sagge
And well bestrutted bees sweet bagge :
Gladding his pallat with some store
Of emit eggs ; what wo'd he more ?
But beards of mice, a newt's stew'd thigh,
A bloated earewig, and a flie ;
With the red-capt worme, that's shut
Within the concave of a nut,
Browne as his tooth.   A little moth,
Late fatned in a piece of cloth :
With withered cherries ; mandrakes eares ;
Moles eyes ; to these, the slain stags teares :
The unctuous dewlaps of a snaile ;
The broke-heart of a nightingale
Ore-come in musicke ; with a wine,
Ne're ravisht from the flattering vine,
But gently prest from the soft side
Of the most sweet and dainty bride,
Brought in a dainty daizie, which
He fully quaffs up to bewitch
His blood to height ; this done, commended
Grace by his priest ; *The feast is ended.*

—ᗯᐯᗯ—

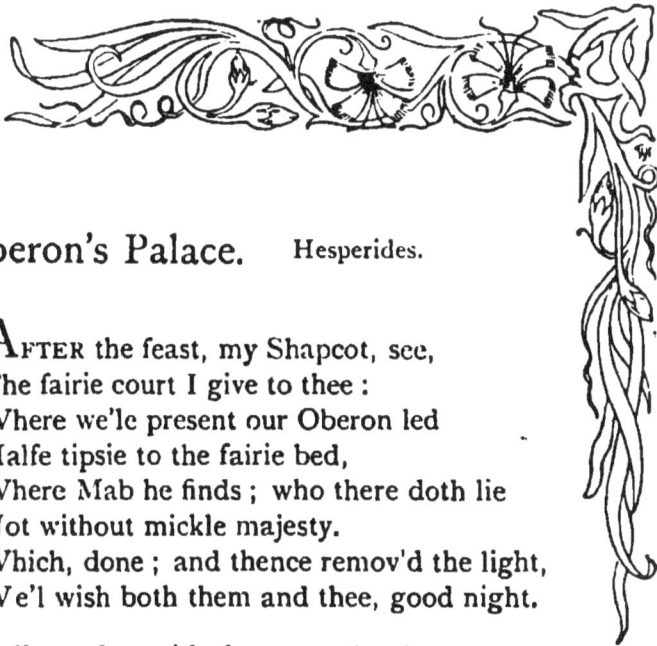

Oberon's Palace. Hesperides.

AFTER the feast, my Shapcot, see,
The fairie court I give to thee :
Where we'le present our Oberon led
Halfe tipsie to the fairie bed,
Where Mab he finds ; who there doth lie
Not without mickle majesty.
Which, done ; and thence remov'd the light,
We'l wish both them and thee, good night.

Full as a bee with thyme, and red,
As cherry harvest, now high fed
For lust and action ; on he'l go,
To lye with Mab, though all say no.
Lust ha's no eares ; he's sharpe as thorn ;
And fretfull, carries hay in's horne,
And lightning in his eyes ; and flings
Among the elves, if mov'd, the stings
Of peltish wasps ; we'l know his guard
Kings though th'are hated, will be fear'd.
Wine lead him on.   Thus to a grove,
Sometimes devoted unto Love,
Tinseld with twilight, he, and they
Lead by the shine of snails ; a way
Beat with their num'rous feet, which by
Many a neat perplexity,
Many a turn, and man' a crosse-
Track they redeem a bank of mosse

Lyric Poems.

Spungie and swelling, and farre more
Soft then the finest Lemster ore.
Mildly disparkling, like those fiers,
Which break from the injeweld tyres
Of curious brides ; or like those mites
Of candi'd dew in moony nights.
Upon this convex, all the flowers,
Nature begets by th' sun, and showers,
Are to a wilde digestion brought,
As if Love's sampler here was wrought :
Or Citherea's ceston, which
All with temptation doth bewitch.
Sweet aires move here ; and more divine
Made by the breath of great ey'd-kine,
Who as they lowe empearl with milk
The four-leav'd grasse, or mosse-like silk.
The breath of munkies met to mix
With musk-flies, are th' aromaticks.
Which cense this arch ; and here and there,
And farther off, and every where,
Throughout that brave mosaick yard
Those picks or diamonds in the card :
With peeps of harts, of club and spade,
Are here most neatly inter-laid.
Many a counter, many a die,
Half rotten, and without an eye,
Lies here abouts ; and for to pave
The excellency of this cave,
Squirrils' and children's teeth late shed,
Are neatly here enchequered.
With brownest toadstones, and the gum
That shines upon the blewer plum.
The nails faln off by whit-flawes : Art's
Wise hand enchasing here those warts,

Herrick.

Which we to others, from our selves,
Sell, and brought hither by the elves.
The tempting mole, stoln from the neck
Of the shic virgin, seems to deck
The holy entrance ; where within
The roome is hung with the blew skin
Of shifted snake : enfreez'd throughout
With eyes of peacocks trains, and trout-
flies curious wings ; and these among
Those silver-pence, that cut the tongue
Of the red infant, neatly hung.
The glow-wormes eyes ; the shining scales
Of silv'rie fish ; wheat-strawes, the snailes
Soft candle-light ; the kitling's eyne ;
Corrupted wood ; serve here for shine.
No glaring light of bold-fac't day,
Or other over radiant ray
Ransacks this roome ; but what weak beams
Can make reflected from these jems,
And multiply ; such is the light,
But ever doubtfull day, or night.
By this quaint taper-light he winds
His errours up ; and now he finds
His moon-tann'd Mab, as somewhat sick,
And, Love knowes, tender as a chick.
Upon six plump dandillions, high-
Rear'd, lyes her elvish-majestie :
Whose woollie-bubbles seem'd to drowne
Hir Mab-ship in obedient downe.
For either sheet, was spread the caule
That doth the infants face enthrall,
When it is born : (by some enstyl'd
The luckie omen of the child)
And next to these two blankets ore-

Lyric Poems.

Cast of the finest gossamore.
And then a rug of carded wooll,
Which, spunge-like drinking in the dull-
Light of the moon, seem'd to comply,
Cloud-like, the daintie deitie.
Thus soft she lies : and over-head
A spinners circle is bespread,
With cob-web-curtains : from the roof
So neatly sunck, as that no proof
Of any tackling can declare
What gives it hanging in the aire.
The fringe about this, are those threds
Broke at the losse of maiden-heads :
And all behung with these pure pearls,
Dropt from the eyes of ravisht girles
Or writhing brides ; when, panting, they
Give unto love the straiter way.
For musick now ; he has the cries
Of fained-lost-virginities ;
The which the elves make to excite
A more unconquer'd appetite.
The king's undrest ; and now upon
The gnats-watch-word the elves are gone.
And now the bed, and Mab possest
Of this great-little-kingly-guest.
We'll nobly think, what's to be done,
He'll do no doubt ; *This flax is spun.*

—∿∿∿—

Herrick.

The Beggar to Mab, the Fairie Queen.

"Huckson" (l. 11), the hock. Hesperides.

PLEASE your grace, from out your store,
Give an almes to one that's poore,
That your mickle, may have more.
Black I'm grown for want of meat ;
Give me then an ant to eate ;
Or the cleft eare of a mouse
Over-sowr'd in drinke of souce :
Or, sweet lady, reach to me
The abdomen of a bee ;
Or commend a crickets-hip,
Or his huckson, to my scrip.
Give for bread, a little bit
Of a pease, that 'gins to chit,
And my full thanks take for it.
Floure of fuz-balls, that's too good
For a man in needy-hood :
But the meal of mill-dust can
Well content a craving man.
Any orts the elves refuse
Well will serve the beggars use.
But if this may seem too much
For an almes ; then give me such
Little bits, that nestle there
In the pris'ners panier.
So a blessing light upon
You, and mighty Oberon :
That your plenty last till when,
I return your almes agen.

Stool-Ball.

Stool-ball was a kind of primitive cricket, played by two. Hesperides.

At stool-ball, Lucia, let us play,
For sugar-cakes and wine ;
Or for a transie let us pay,
The losse or thine, or mine.

If thou, my deere, a winner be
At trundling of the ball,
The wager thou shalt have, and me,
And my misfortunes all.

But if, my sweetest, I shall get,
Then I desire but this ;
That likewise I may pay the bet,
And have for all a kisse.

—⁓⁓⁓—

His Charge to Julia :

"At his Death." Hesperides.

Dearest of thousands, now the time drawes
neere,
That with my lines, my life must full-stop here.
Cut off thy haires ; and let thy teares be shed
Over my turfe, when I am buried.
Then for effusions, let none wanting be,
Or other rites that doe belong to me ;
As Love shall helpe thee, when thou do'st go
hence
Unto thy everlasting residence.

Herrick.

The Bad Season makes the Poet Sad.

Hesperides.

Dull to my selfe, and almost dead to these
My many fresh and fragrant mistresses :
Lost to all musick now ; since every thing
Puts on the semblance here of sorrowing.
Sick is the land to'th' heart ; and doth endure
More dangerous faintings by her desp'rate cure.
But if that golden age wo'd come again,
And Charles here rule, as he before did raign ;
If smooth and unperplext the seasons were,
As when the sweet Maria lived here :
I sho'd delight to have my curles halfe drown'd
In Tyrian dewes, and head with roses crown'd.
And once more yet (ere I am laid out dead)
Knock at a starre with my exalted head.

His Age.

"Dedicated to his peculiar friend, M. John Wickes, under the name of Posthumus." Hesperides. "Pricket" (v. 18), a young stag.

Aн Posthumus ! our yeares hence flye,
And leave no sound ; nor piety,
      Or prayers, or vow
Can keepe the wrinkle from the brow :
      But we must on,
As Fate do's lead or draw us ; none,
None, Posthumus, co'd ere decline
The doome of cruell Proserpine.

The pleasing wife, the house, the ground
Must all be left, no one plant found
      To follow thee,
Save only the curst-cipresse tree :
      A merry mind
Looks forward, scornes what's left behind :
Let's live, my Wickes, then, while we may,
And here enjoy our holiday.

W'ave seen the past-best times, and these
Will nere return, we see the seas,
      And moons to wain ;
But they fill up their ebbs again :
      But vanisht man,
Like to a lilly-lost, nere can,
Nere can repullulate, or bring
His dayes to see a second spring.

Herrick.

But on we must, and thither tend,
Where Anchus and rich Tullus blend
        Their sacred seed :
Thus has infernall Jove decreed ;
        We must be made,
Ere long, a song, ere long, a shade.
Why then, since life to us is short,
Lets make it full up, by our sport.

Crown we our heads with roses then,
And 'noint with Tirian balme ; for when
        We two are dead,
The world with us is buried.
        Then live we free,
As is the air, and let us be
Our own fair wind, and mark each one
Day with the white and luckie stone.

We are not poore ; although we have
No roofs of cedar, nor our brave
        Baiæ, nor keep
Account of such a flock of sheep ;
        Nor bullocks fed
To lard the shambles : barbels bred
To kisse our hands, nor do we wish
For Pollio's lampries in our dish.

If we can meet, and so conferre,
Both by a shining salt-seller ;
        And have our roofe,
Although not archt, yet weather proofe,
        And seeling free,
From that cheape candle baudery :
We'le eate our beane with that full mirth,
As we were lords of all the earth.

Lyric Poems.

Well then, on what seas we are tost,
Our comfort is, we can't be lost.
        Let the winds drive
Our barke; yet she will keepe alive
        Amidst the deepes;
'Tis constancy, my Wickes, which keepes
The pinnace up; which though she erres
I'th' seas, she saves her passengers.

Say, we must part, sweet mercy blesse,
Us both i'th' sea, camp, wildernesse,
        Can we so farre
Stray, to become lesse circular,
        Then we are now?
No, no, that selfe same heart, that vow,
Which made us one, shall ne'r undoe;
Or ravell so, to make us two.

Live in thy peace; as for my selfe,
When I am bruised on the shelfe
        Of time, and show
My locks behung with frost and snow:
        When with the reume,
The cough, the ptisick, I consume
Unto an almost nothing; then,
The ages fled, Ile call agen:

And with a teare compare these last
Lame, and bad times, with those are past,
        While Baucis by,
My old leane wife, shall kisse it dry:
        And so we'l sit
By 'th'fire, foretelling snow and slit,
And weather by our aches, grown
Now old enough to be our own

Herrick.

True calendars, as pusses eare
Washt o'er, to tell what change is neare :
            Then to asswage
The gripings of the chine by age ;
            I'le call my young
Iülus to sing such a song
I made upon my Julia's brest ;
And of her blush at such a feast.

Then shall he read that flowre of mine
Enclos'd within a christall shrine :
            A primrose next ;
A piece, then of a higher text :
            For to beget
In me a more transcendant heate,
Then that insinuating fire,
Which crept into each aged sire.

When the faire Hellen, from her eyes,
Shot forth her loving sorceries :
            At which I'le reare
Mine aged limbs above my chaire :
            And hearing it,
Flutter and crow, as in a fit
Of fresh concupiscence, and cry,
No lust theres like to poetry.

Thus frantick crazie man, God wot,
Ile call to mind things half forgot :
            And oft between,
Repeat the times that I have seen !
            Thus ripe with tears,
And twisting my Iülus hairs ;
Doting, Ile weep and say, In truth,
Baucis, these were my sins of youth.

Lyric Poems.

Then next Ile cause my hopefull lad,
If a wild apple can be had,
      To crown the hearth,
Larr thus conspiring with our mirth,
      Then to infuse
Our browner ale into the cruse :
Which sweetly spic't, we'l first carouse
Unto the Genius of the house.

Then the next health to friends of mine,
Loving the brave Burgundian wine,
      High sons of Pith,
Whose fortunes I have frolickt with :
      Such as co'd well
Bear up the magick bough, and spel :
And dancing 'bout the mystick Thyrse,
Give up the just applause to verse :

To those, and then agen to thee
We'l drink, my Wickes, untill we be
      Plump as the cherry,
Though not so fresh, yet full as merry
      As the crickit ;
The untam'd heifer, or the pricket,
Untill our tongues shall tell our ears,
W'are younger by a score of years.

Thus, till we see the fire lesse shine
From th' embers, then the kitlings eyne,
      We'l still sit up,
Sphering about the wassail cup,
      To all those times,
Which gave me honour for my rhimes,
The cole once spent, we'l then to bed,
Farre more then night bewearied.

Herrick.

His Returne to London.

From the dull confines of the drooping west,
To see the day spring from the pregnant east,
Ravisht in spirit, I come, nay more, I flie
To thee, blest place of my nativitie !
Thus, thus with hallowed foot I touch the
　　ground,
With thousand blessings by thy fortune
　　crown'd.
O fruitfull Genius ! that bestowest here
An everlasting plenty, yeere by yeere.
O place ! O people ! manners ! fram'd to
　　please
All nations, customes, kindreds, languages !
I am a free-born Roman ; suffer then,
That I amongst you live a citizen.
London my home is : though by hard fate sent
Into a long and irksome banishment ;
Yet since cal'd back ; henceforward let me be,
O native countrey, repossest by thee !
For, rather then I'le to the west return,
I'le beg of thee first here to have mine urn.
Weak I am grown, and must in short time fall ;
Give thou my sacred reliques buriall.

—⁓⋁⋁⋁⁓—

His Winding Sheet.

COME thou, who art the wine, and wit
    Of all I've writ :
The grace, the glorie, and the best
    Piece of the rest.
Thou art of what I did intend
    The all, and end.
And what was made, was made to meet
    Thee, thee my sheet.
Come then, and be to my chast side
    Both bed, and bride.
We two, as reliques left, will have
    One rest, one grave.
And, hugging close, we will not feare
    Lust entring here :
Where all desires are dead, or cold
    As is the mould :
And all affections are forgot,
    Or trouble not.
Here, here the slaves and pris'ners be
    From shackles free :
And weeping widowes long opprest
    Doe here find rest.
The wronged client ends his lawes
    Here, and his cause.
Here those long suits of Chancery lie
    Quiet, or die :
And all Star-chamber-bils doe cease,
    Or hold their peace.

Herrick.

Here needs no court for our request,
        Where all are best ;
All wise ; all equall ; and all just
        Alike i'th' dust.
Nor need we here to feare the frowne
        Of Court, or Crown.
Where Fortune bears no sway o're things,
        There all are Kings.
In this securer place we'l keep,
        As lull'd asleep ;
Or for a little time we'l lye,
        As robes laid by ;
To be another day re-worne,
        Turn'd, but not torn :
Or like old testaments ingrost,
        Lockt up, not lost :
And for a while lye here conceal'd,
        To be reveal'd
Next, at that great Platonick yeere,
        And then meet here.

—⁓⋌⋋⋌⋋⁓—

The Funerall
Rites of the   Hesperides.
Rose.

The rose was sick, and smiling di'd ;
And, being to be sanctifi'd,
About the bed, there sighing stood
The sweet, and flowrie sisterhood.
Some hung the head, while some did bring
(To wash her) water from the spring.

Lyric Poems.

Some laid her forth, while others wept,
But all a solemne fast there kept.
The holy sisters some among
The sacred dirge and trentall sung.
But ah ! what sweets smelt every where,
As Heaven had spent all perfumes there.
At last, when prayers for the dead,
And rites were all accomplished ;
They, weeping, spread a lawnie loome,
And clos'd her up, as in a tombe.

—⁓⋁⋀⋁⋀⁓—

To the Rose.   Song. Hesperides.

GOE, happy rose, and enterwove
　　With other flowers, bind my love.
　　Tell her too, she must not be,
　　Longer flowing, longer free,
　　That so oft has fetter'd me.

Say, if she's fretfull, I have bands
Of pearle, and gold, to bind her hands :
　　Tell her, if she struggle still,
　　I have mirtle rods, at will,
　　For to tame, though not to kill.

Take thou my blessing, thus, and goe,
And tell her this, but doe not so,
　　Lest a handsome anger flye,
　　Like a lightning, from her eye,
　　And burn thee up, as well as I.

—⁓⋁⋀⋁⋀⁓—

An Ode for Ben Johnson.

Aᴴ Ben !
Say how, or when
Shall we thy guests
Meet at those lyrick feasts,
Made at the Sun,
The Dog, the triple Tunne?
Where we such clusters had,
As made us nobly wild, not mad;
And yet each verse of thine
Out-did the meate, out-did the frolick wine.

My Ben !
Or come agen :
Or send to us,
Thy wits great over-plus ;
But teach us yet
Wisely to husband it ;
Lest we that tallent spend :
And having once brought to an end
That precious stock ; the store
Of such a wit the world sho'd have no more.

—⋀⋀⋀—

His Prayer to Ben Johnson.

Hesperides.

WHEN I a verse shall make,
Know I have praid thee,
For old religions sake,
Saint Ben, to aide me.

Make the way smooth for me,
When I, thy Herrick,
Honouring thee, on my knee
Offer my lyrick.

Candles Ile give to thee,
And a new altar ;
And thou, Saint Ben, shalt be
Writ in my Psalter.

—᭴᭴᭴᭴—

A Bacchanalian Verse.

Hesperides.

FILL me a mighty bowle
Up to the brim :
That I may drink
Unto my Johnsons soule.

Crowne it agen agen ;
And thrice repeat
That happy heat ;
To drink to thee my Ben.

136

Herrick.

Well I can quaffe, I see,
To th' number five,
Or nine ; but thrive
In frenzie ne'r like thee.

—∿∿∿—

Upon the Troublesome Times.

Hesperides.

O ! times most bad,
Without the scope
Of hope
Of better to be had !

Where shall I goe,
Or whither run
To shun
This publique overthrow ?

No places are
(This I am sure)
Secure
In this our wasting warre.

Some storms w'ave past ;
Yet we must all
Down fall,
And perish at the last.

—∿∿∿—

Lyric Poems.

On Himselfe.

"Trentalls," Masses for the Dead, in sets of thirty. (Italian, *Trenta*.) Hesperides.

Ile sing no more, nor will I longer write
Of that sweet lady, or that gallant knight :
Ile sing no more of frosts, snowes, dews and
    showers ;
No more of groves, meades, springs, and
    wreaths of flowers :
Ile write no more, nor will I tell or sing
Of Cupid, and his wittie coozning :
Ile sing no more of death, or shall the grave
No more my dirges, and my trentalls have.

—⋏⋀⋁⋏—

An Hymne to the Muses.

Hesperides.

Honour to you who sit !
    Neere to the well of wit ;
    And drink your fill of it.

Glory and worship be !
To you, sweet maids (thrice three)
Who still inspire me.

And teach me how to sing
Unto the lyrick string
My measures ravishing.

Then while I sing your praise,
My priest-hood crown with bayes
Green, to the end of dayes.

138

Herrick.

Not every Day fit for Verse.

Hesperides.

'TIS not ev'ry day, that I
Fitted am to prophesie :
No, but when the spirit fils
The fantastick pannicles
Full of fier ; then I write
As the Godhead doth indite.
Thus inrag'd, my lines are hurl'd,
Like the Sybells, through the world.
Look how next the holy fier
Either slakes, or doth retire ;
So the fancie cooles, till when
That brave spirit comes agen.

—ᴡᴡᴡ—

Anacreontick Verse.

Hesperides.

BRISK methinks I am, and fine,
When I drinke my capring wine :
Then to love I do encline,
When I drinke my wanton wine :
And I wish all maidens mine,
When I drinke my sprightly wine :
Well I sup, and well I dine,
When I drinke my frolick wine :
But I languish, lowre, and pine,
When I want my fragrant wine.

139

To be Merry. Hesperides.

LETS now take our time ;
While w'are in our prime ;
And old, old age is a farre off :
For the evill evill dayes
Will come on apace ;
Before we can be aware of.

—◦◦◦◦◦—

The Bride-Cake. Hesperides.

THIS day, my Julia, thou must make
For mistresse bride, the wedding cake :
Knead but the dow, and it will be
To paste of almonds turn'd by thee :
Or kisse it thou, but once, or twice,
And for the bride-cake ther'l be spice.

—◦◦◦◦◦—

Charmes. Hesperides.

THIS Ile tell ye by the way,
Maidens, when ye leavens lay,
Crosse your dow, and your dispatch,
Will be better for your batch.

Herrick.

IN the morning when ye rise,
Wash your hands, and cleanse your eyes.
Next be sure ye have a care,
To disperse the water farre.
For as farre as that doth light,
So farre keepes the evill spright.

IF ye feare to be affrighted
When ye are, by chance, benighted :
In your pocket for a trust,
Carrie nothing but a crust :
For that holy piece of bread
Charmes the danger, and the dread.

—ᴡᴡᴡ—

The Ceremonies for Christmasse Day. Hesperides.

KINDLE the Christmas brand and then
      Till sunne-set, let it burne ;
Which quencht, then lay it up agen,
      Till Christmas next returne.

Part must be kept wherewith to teend
      The Christmas log next yeare ;
And where 'tis safely kept, the fiend,
      Can do no mischiefe, there.

Ceremonies for Candlemasse Eve.

Hesperides.

I.

Down with the rosemary and bayes,
Down with the misleto ;
Instead of holly, now up-raise
The greener box, for show.

The holly hitherto did sway ;
Let box now domineere ;
Untill the dancing Easter-day,
Or Easters eve appeare.

Then youthfull box which now hath grace,
Your houses to renew ;
Grown old, surrender must his place,
Unto the crisped yew.

When yew is out, then birch comes in,
And many flowers beside ;
Both of a fresh, and fragrant kinne
To honour Whitsontide.

Green rushes then, and sweetest bents,
With cooler oken boughs ;
Come in for comely ornaments,
To re-adorn the house.
Thus times do shift ; each thing his turne do's
hold ;
New things succeed, as former things grow old.

II.

Down with the rosemary, and so
Down with the baies, and misletoe :
Down with the holly, ivie, all,
Wherewith ye drest the Christmas hall :
That so the superstitious find
No one least branch there left behind :
For look, how many leaves there be
Neglected there, maids, trust to me,
So many goblins you shall see.

—ᴡᴡᴡ—

To the Genius of his House.

Hesperides.

Command the roofe, great Genius, and from
    thence
Into this house powre downe thy influence,
That through each room a golden pipe may run
Of living water by thy benizon.
Fulfill the larders, and with strengthning bread
Be evermore these bynns replenished.
Next, like a bishop consecrate my ground,
That luckie fairies here may dance their round :
And after that, lay downe some silver pence,
The masters charge and care to recompence.
Charme then the chambers ; make the beds for
    ease,
More then for peevish pining sicknesses.
Fix the foundation fast, and let the roofe
Grow old with time, but yet keep weather-
    proofe.

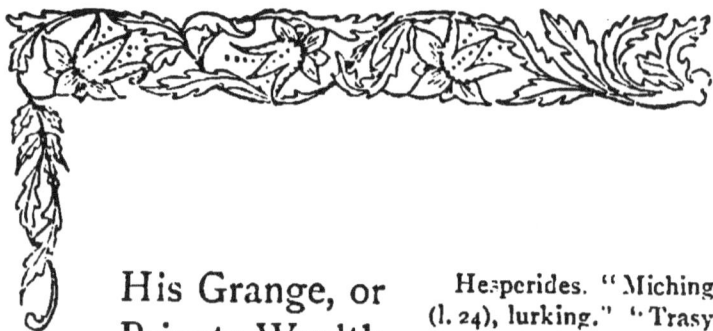

His Grange, or Private Wealth.

Hesperides. " Miching (l. 24), lurking." " Trasy (l. 26), spaniel."

THOUGH clock,
To tell how night drawes hence, I've none,
A cock,
I have, to sing how day drawes on.
I have
A maid, my Prew, by good luck sent,
To save
That little, Fates me gave or lent.
A hen
I keep, which creeking day by day,
Tells when
She goes her long white egg to lay.
A goose
I have, which, with a jealous care,
Lets loose
Her tongue, to tell what danger's neare.
A lamb
I keep (tame) with my morsells fed,
Whose dam
An orphan left him (lately dead.)
A cat
I keep, that playes about my house,
Grown fat,

With eating many a miching mouse.
                    To these
A trasy I do keep, whereby
                    I please
The more my rurall privacie :
                    Which are
But toyes, to give my heart some ease :
                    Where care
None is, slight things do lightly please.

—wwww—

A Beucolick :   Or, Discourse of Neat-
                herds.   Hesperides.
                " Steerling," diminutive
                of steer.

1 COME, blithefull neatherds, let us lay
  A wager, who the best shall play,
  Of thee, or I, the roundelay,
  That fits the businesse of the day.

Chor. And Lallage the judge shall be,
  To give the prize to thee, or me.

2 Content, begin, and I will bet
  A heifer smooth, and black as jet,
  In every part alike compleat,
  And wanton as a kid as yet.

Chor. And Lallage, with cow-like eyes,
  Shall be disposeresse of the prize.

1 Against thy heifer, I will here
  Lay to thy stake a lustie steere,
  With gilded hornes, and burnisht cleere.

10 K   145

Lyric Poems.

Chor. Why then begin, and let us heare
The soft, the sweet, the mellow note
That gently purles from eithers oat.

2 The stakes are laid : let's now apply
Each one to make his melody :

Lal. The equall umpire shall be I,
Who'l hear, and so judge righteously.

Chor. Much time is spent in prate ; begin,
And sooner play, the sooner win.
[*He playes.*
1 That's sweetly touch't, I must confesse :
Thou art a man of worthinesse :
But hark how I can now expresse
My love unto my neatherdesse.
[*He sings.*
Chor. A suger'd note ! and sound as sweet
As kine, when they at milking meet.

1 Now for to win thy heifer faire,
I'le strike thee such a nimble ayre,
That thou shalt say, thy selfe, 'tis rare ;
And title me without compare.

Chor. Lay by a while your pipes, and rest,
Since both have here deserved best.

2 To get thy steerling, once again,
I'le play thee such another strain ;
That thou shalt swear, my pipe do's
raigne
Over thine oat, as soveraigne. [*He sings.*

Chor. And Lallage shall tell by this,
    Whose now the prize and wager is.

  1 Give me the prize : 2. The day is mine :
  1 Not so ; my pipe has silenc't thine :
    And hadst thou wager'd twenty kine,
    They were mine own. *Lal.* In love
    combine.

Chor. And lay we down our pipes together,
    As wearie, not o'recome by either.

—∿∿∿—

Lacon and Thyrsis :

A Bucolick betwixt Two. Hesperides. "Neat-heardesse," cow-herdess.

Lacon. FOR a kiss or two, confesse,
    What doth cause this pensiveness,
    Thou most lovely neat-heardesse?
    Why so lonely on the hill?
    Why thy pipe by thee so still,
    That ere while was heard so shrill
    Tell me, do thy kine now fail
    To fulfill the milkin-paile?
    Say, what is't that thou do'st aile?

Thyr. None of these ; but out, alas !
    A mischance is come to pass,
    And I'le tell thee what it was :
    See mine eyes are weeping ripe,

Lacon. Tell, and I'le lay down my pipe.

Lyric Poems.

Thyr. I have lost my lovely steere,
That to me was far more deer
Then these kine, which I milke here.
Broad of fore-head, large of eye,
Party colour'd like a pie ;
Smooth in each limb as a die ;
Clear of hoof, and clear of horn ;
Sharply pointed as a thorn :
With a neck by yoke unworn.
From the which hung down by strings,
Balls of cowslips, daisie rings,
Enterplac't with ribbanings.
Faultless every way for shape ;
Not a straw co'd him escape ;
Ever gamesome as an ape :
But yet harmless as a sheep.
Pardon, Lacon, if I weep ;
Tears will spring, where woes are deep.
Now, ai me ! ai me ! Last night
Came a mad dog, and did bite,
I, and kil'd my dear delight.

Lacon. Alack, for grief !

Thyr. But I'le be brief.
Hence I must, for time doth call
Me, and my sad play-mates all,
To his ev'ning funerall.
Live long, Lacon, so adew !

Lacon. Mournfull maid, farewell to you ;
Earth afford ye flowers to strew.

Herrick.

A Dialogue.

" Betwixt himselfe and Mistresse Eliza: Wheeler, under the name of Amarillis." Hesperides. "Maunds (l. 7), a two-handled basket."

My dearest love, since thou wilt go,
　And leave me here behind thee ;
For love or pitie let me know
　The place where I may find thee.

Amaril. In country meadowes pearl'd with dew,
　And set about with lillies ;
There filling maunds with cowslips,you
　May find your Amarillis.

Her.　What have the meades to do with thee,
　Or with thy youthfull houres ?
Live thou at court,where thou mayst be
　The queen of men, not flowers.

Let country wenches make 'em fine
　With poesies, since 'tis fitter
For thee with richest jemmes to shine,
　And like the starres to glitter.

Amaril. You set too high a rate upon
　A shepheardess so homely.
Her.　Believe it, dearest, ther's not one
　I'th' court that's halfe so comly.

I prithee stay. *Amaril.* I must away ;
　Lets kiss first, then we'l sever.
Ambo.　And though we bid adieu to day,
　Wee shall not part for ever.

Lyric Poems.

Upon Love : By way of Question and Answer. Hesperides.

I BRING ye Love.   *Quest.* What will Love do?
    Ans. Like, and dislike ye :
I bring ye Love : *Quest.* What will Love do?
    Ans. Stroake ye to strike ye.
I bring ye Love : *Quest.* What will Love do ?
    Ans. Love will be-foole ye :
I bring ye Love : *Quest.* What will Love do ?
    Ans. Heate ye to coole ye :
I bring ye Love : *Quest.* What will Love do ?
    Ans. Love gifts will send ye :
I bring ye Love : *Quest.* What will Love do ?
    Ans. Stock ye to spend ye :
I bring ye Love : *Quest.* What will Love do ?
    Ans. Love will fulfill ye :
I bring ye Love : *Quest.* What will Love do ?
    Ans. Kisse ye, to kill ye.

—∿∿∿—

To Oenone. Hesperides.

WHAT conscience, say, is it in thee
    When I a heart had one,
To take away that heart from me,
    And to retain thy own ?

For shame or pitty now encline
    To play a loving part ;
Either to send me kindly thine,
    Or give me back my heart.

Herrick.

Covet not both ; but if thou dost
    Resolve to part with neither ;
Why ! yet to shew that thou art just,
    Take me and mine together.

—⋀⋀⋀—

The Primrose.

One of the poems set to music by Lawes. Hesperides.

Aske me why I send you here
    This sweet Infanta of the yeere?
    Aske me why I send to you
This primrose, thus bepearl'd with dew?
    I will whisper to your eares,
The sweets of love are mixt with tears.

    Ask me why this flower do's show
So yellow-green, and sickly too?
    Ask me why the stalk is weak
And bending, yet it doth not break?
    I will answer, These discover
What fainting hopes are in a lover.

—⋀⋀⋀—

A Thanksgiving to God :

LORD, Thou hast given me a cell
    Wherein to dwell ;
A little house, whose humble roof
    Is weather-proof ;
Under the sparres of which I lie
    Both soft, and drie ;
Where Thou my chamber for to ward
    Hast set a guard
Of harmlesse thoughts, to watch and keep
    Me, while I sleep.
Low is my porch, as is my fate,
    Both void of state ;
And yet the threshold of my doore
    Is worn by th' poore,
Who thither come, and freely get
    Good words, or meat :
Like as my parlour, so my hall
    And kitchin's small :
A little butterie, and therein
    A little byn,
Which keeps my little loafe of bread
    Unchipt, unflead :
Some brittle sticks of thorne or briar
    Make me a fire,

Herrick.

Close by whose living coale I sit,
            And glow like it.
Lord, I confesse too, when I dine,
            The pulse is Thine,
And all those other bits, that bee
            There plac'd by Thee ;
The worts, the purslain, and the messe
            Of water-cresse,
Which of thy kindnesse Thou has sent ;
            And my content
Makes those, and my beloved beet,
            To be more sweet.
'Tis thou that crown'st my glittering hearth
            With guiltlesse mirth ;
And giv'st me wassaile bowles to drink,
            Spic'd to the brink.
Lord, 'tis thy plenty-dropping hand,
            That soiles my land ;
And giv'st me, for my bushell sowne,
            Twice ten for one :
Thou mak'st my teeming hen to lay
            Her egg each day :
Besides my healthfull ewes to beare
            Me twins each yeare :
The while the conduits of my kine
            Run creame, for wine.
All these, and better Thou dost send
            Me, to this end,
That I should render, for my part,
            A thankfull heart ;
Which, fir'd with incense, I resigne,
            As wholly Thine ;
But the acceptance, that must be,
            My Christ, by Thee.

The Bell-man. Hesperides.

Along the dark, and silent night,
With my lantern, and my light,
And the tinkling of my bell,
Thus I walk, and this I tell :
Death and dreadfulnesse call on,
To the gen'rall session ;
To whose dismall barre, we there
All accompts must come to cleere :
Scores of sins w'ave made here many,
Wip't out few, God knowes, if any.
Rise, ye debters, then, and fall
To make paiment, while I call.
Ponder this, when I am gone ;
By the clock 'tis almost one.

—⁓⁓—

Proof to no Purpose. Hesperides.

You see this gentle streame, that glides,
Shov'd on, by quick succeeding tides :
Trie if this sober streame you can
Follow to th' wilder ocean :
And see, if there it keeps unspent
In that congesting element.
Next, from that world of waters, then
By poares and cavernes back agen

Herrick.

Induc't that inadultrate same
Streame to the spring from whence it came.
This with a wonder when ye do,
As easie, and els easier too :
Then may ye recollect the graines
Of my particular remaines ;
After a thousand lusters hurld,
By ruffling winds, about the world.

—wWw—

To finde God.   Noble Numbers.

Weigh me the fire ; or canst thou find
- A way to measure out the wind ;
Distinguish all those floods that are
Mixt in that watrie theater ;
And tast thou them as saltlesse there,
As in their channell first they were.
Tell me the people that do keep
Within the kingdomes of the deep ;
Or fetch me back that cloud againe,
Beshiver'd into seeds of raine ;
Tell me the motes, dust, sands, and speares
Of corn, when Summer shakes his eares ;
Shew me that world of starres, and whence
They noiselesse spill their influence :
This if thou canst ; then shew me Him
That rides the glorious Cherubim.

—wWw—

Lyric Poems.

His Prayer for Absolution.

Noble Numbers.

FOR those my unbaptized rhimes,
Writ in my wild unhallowed times ;
For every sentence, clause, and word,
That's not inlaid with Thee, my Lord,
Forgive me, God, and blot each line
Out of my book, that is not Thine.
But if, 'mongst all, Thou find'st here one
Worthy thy benediction ;
That one of all the rest, shall be
The glory of my work, and me.

—⁓⁓⁓—

His Letanie :

"To the Holy Spirit."
Noble Numbers.

IN the houre of my distresse,
When temptations me oppresse,
And when I my sins confesse,
    Sweet Spirit, comfort me !

When I lie within my bed,
Sick in heart, and sick in head,
And with doubts discomforted,
    Sweet Spirit, comfort me !

When the house doth sigh and weep,
And the world is drown'd in sleep,
Yet mine eyes the watch do keep ;
    Sweet Spirit, comfort me !

156

Herrick.

When the artlesse doctor sees
No one hope, but of his fees,
And his skill runs on the lees ;
   Sweet Spirit, comfort me!

When his potion and his pill,
His, or none, or little skill,
Meet for nothing, but to kill ;
   Sweet Spirit, comfort me !

When the passing-bell doth tole,
And the furies in a shole
Come to fright a parting soule ;
   Sweet Spirit, comfort me !

When the tapers now burne blew,
And the comforters are few,
And that number more then true ;
   Sweet Spirit, comfort me !

When the priest his last hath praid,
And I nod to what is said,
'Cause my speech is now decaid ;
   Sweet Spirit, comfort me !

When, God knowes, I'm tost about,
Either with despaire, or doubt ;
Yet before the glasse be out,
   Sweet Spirit, comfort me !

When the tempter me pursu'th
With the sins of all my youth,
And halfe damns me with untruth ;
   Sweet Spirit, comfort me !

Lyric Poems.

When the flames and hellish cries
Fright mine eares, and fright mine eyes,
And all terrors me surprize ;
      Sweet Spirit, comfort me !

When the judgment is reveal'd,
And that open'd which was seal'd,
When to Thee I have appeal'd ;
      Sweet Spirit, comfort me !

—✕✕✕—

Honours are Hindrances.

Noble Numbers.

Give me honours : what are these,
But the pleasing hindrances ?
Stiles, and stops, and stayes, that come
In the way 'twixt me, and home :
Cleer the walk, and then shall I
To my heaven lesse run, then flie.

—✕✕✕—

To His Saviour, a Child.

A present, by a child.
Noble Numbers.

Go, prettie child, and beare this flower
Unto thy little Saviour ;
And tell Him, by that bud now blown,
He is the Rose of Sharon known :
When thou hast said so, stick it there
Upon His bibb, or stomacher :
And tell Him, for good handsell too,
That thou hast brought a whistle new,

158

Herrick.

Made of a clean strait oaten reed,
To charme His cries, at time of need :
Tell Him, for corall, thou hast none ;
But if thou hadst, He sho'd have one ;
But poore thou art, and knowne to be
Even as monilesse, as He.
Lastly, if thou canst win a kisse
From those mellifluous lips of His ;
Then never take a second on,
To spoile the first impression.

—⁓⁓⁓—

To His Sweet Saviour.

Night hath no wings, to him that cannot
    sleep ;
And Time seems then, not for to flie, but
    creep ;
Slowly her chariot drives, as if that she
Had broke her wheele, or crackt her axeltree.
Just so it is with me, who list'ning, pray
The winds, to blow the tedious night away ;
That I might see the cheerfull peeping day.
Sick is my heart ! O Saviour ! do Thou please
To make my bed soft in my sicknesses :
Lighten my candle, so that I beneath
Sleep not for ever in the vaults of death :
Let me Thy voice betimes i'th' morning heare ;
Call, and I'le come : say Thou, the when, and
    where :
Draw me, but first, and after Thee I'le run,
And make no one stop, till my race be done.

His Creed.

I DO believe, that die I must,
And be return'd from out my dust :
I do believe, that when I rise,
Christ I shall see, with these same eyes :
I do believe, that I must come,
With others, to the dreadfull doome :
I do believe the bad must goe
From thence, to everlasting woe :
I do believe, the good, and I,
Shall live with Him eternally :
I do believe, I shall inherit
Heaven, by Christs mercies, not my merit :
I do believe, the One in Three,
And Three in perfect Unitie :
Lastly, that JESUS is a deed
Of gift from God : and heres my creed.

—∿∿—

Grace for a Child.

HERE a little child I stand,
Heaving up my either hand ;
Cold as paddocks though they be,
Here I lift them up to Thee,
For a benizon to fall
On our meat, and on us all. Amen.

A Christmas Caroll.

"Sung to the king in the presence at White-Hall. The musicall part was composed by M. Henry Lawes." Noble Numbers.

Chor. WHAT sweeter musick can we bring,
Then a caroll, for to sing
The birth of this our heavenly King?
Awake the voice! awake the string!
Heart, eare, and eye, and every thing
Awake! the while the active finger
Runs division with the singer.
   [*From the flourish they came to the song.*

1 Dark and dull night, flie hence away,
And give the honour to this day,
That sees December turn'd to May.

2 If we may ask the reason, say;
The why, and wherefore all things here
Seem like the spring-time of the yeere?

3 Why do's the chilling winters morne
Smile, like a field beset with corne?
Or smell, like to a meade new-shorne,
Thus, on the sudden? 4. Come and see
The cause, why things thus fragrant be:
'Tis He is borne, whose quickning birth
Gives life and luster, publike mirth,
To heaven, and the under-earth.

Lyric Poems.

Chor. We see Him come, and know him ours,
Who, with His sun - shine, and His
showers,
Turnes all the patient ground to flowers.

1 The darling of the world is come,
And fit it is, we finde a roome
To welcome Him. 2. The nobler part
Of all the house here, is the heart,

Chor. Which we will give Him ; and bequeath
This hollie, and this ivie wreath,
To do Him honour ; who's our King,
And Lord of all this revelling.

—ΛΛΛ—

The New-
Yeeres Gift.

Or Circumcisions Song,
sung to the King in the
presence at White-Hall.
" Composed by M.
Henry Lawes." Noble
Numbers.
" Storax " (l. 8), a
precious gum, used for
incense.

1 PREPARE for songs ; He's come, He's
come ;
And be it sin here to be dumb,
And not with lutes to fill the roome.

2 Cast holy water all about,
And have a care no fire gos out,
But 'cense the porch, and place through-
out.

Herrick.

3 The altars all on fier be ;
  The storax fries ; and ye may see,
  How heart and hand do all agree,
To make things sweet. *Chor.* Yet all less sweet
  then He.

4 Bring Him along, most pious priest,
  And tell us then, when as thou seest
  His gently-gliding, dove-like eyes,
  And hear'st His whimp'ring, and His
    cries ;
  How canst thou this babe circumcise ?

5 Ye must not be more pitifull then wise ;
  For, now unlesse ye see Him bleed,
  Which makes the bapti'me ; 'tis decreed,
The birth is fruitlesse : *Chor.* Then the work
  God speed.

1 Touch gently, gently touch ; and here
  Spring tulips up through all the yeere ;
  And from His sacred bloud, here shed,
May roses grow, to crown His own deare head.

Chor. Back, back again ; each thing is done
  With zeale alike, as 'twas begun ;

  Now singing, homeward let us carrie
  The babe unto His mother Marie ;
  And when we have the child commended
To her warm bosome, then our rites are ended.

—◦◦◦—

An Ode.

"Of the birth of our Saviour." Noble Numbers.

IN numbers, and but these few,
I sing Thy birth, oh JESU !
Thou prettie babie, borne here,
With sup'rabundant scorn here :
Who for Thy princely port here,
　　Hadst for Thy place
　　Of birth, a base
Out-stable for thy court here.

Instead of neat inclosures
Of inter-woven osiers ;
Instead of fragrant posies
Of daffadills, and roses ;
Thy cradle, kingly stranger,
　　As gospell tells,
　　Was nothing els,
But, here, a homely manger.

But we with silks, not cruells,
With sundry precious jewells,
And lilly-work will dresse Thee ;
And as we dispossesse Thee
Of clouts, wee'l make a chamber,
　　Sweet babe, for Thee,
　　Of ivorie,
And plaister'd round with amber.

Herrick.

The Jewes they did disdaine Thee,
But we will entertaine Thee
With glories to await here
Upon Thy princely state here,
And more for love, then pittie.
      From yeere to yeere
      Wee'l make Thee, here,
A free-born of our citie.

—∿∿∿—

To keepe
a True Lent.

Is this a fast, to keep
    The larder leane?
      And cleane
From fat of veales, and sheep?

Is it to quit the dish
    Of flesh, yet still
      To fill
The platter high with fish?

Is it to fast an houre,
    Or rag'd to go,
      Or show
A down-cast look, and sowre?

No : 'tis a fast, to dole
    Thy sheaf of wheat,
      And meat,
Unto the hungry soule.

Lyric Poems.

It is to fast from strife,
From old debate,
And hate ;
To circumcise thy life.

To shew a heart grief-rent ;
To sterve thy sin,
Not bin ;
And that's to keep thy Lent.

—◡◡◡—

The White Island.

Or, Place of the Blest.
Noble Numbers.

IN this world, the Isle of Dreames,
While we sit by sorrowes streames,
Teares and terrors are our theames
Reciting :

But when once from hence we flie,
More and more approaching nigh
Unto young Eternitie
Uniting :

In that whiter island, where
Things are evermore sincere ;
Candor here, and lustre there
Delighting :

There no monstrous fancies shall
Out of hell an horrour call,
To create, or cause at all,
Affrighting.

Herrick.

There in calm and cooling sleep
We our eyes shall never steep ;
But eternall watch shall keep,
                    Attending

Pleasures, such as shall pursue
Me immortaliz'd, and you ;
And fresh joyes, as never too
                    Have ending.

—ᴧᴧ/ᴠ—

Upon Time.   Noble Numbers.

Time was upon
The wing, to flie away ;
    And I cal'd on
Him but a while to stay ;
    But he'd be gone,
For ought that I could say.

He held out then,
A writing, as he went ;
    And askt me, when
False man would be content
    To pay agen,
What God and Nature lent.

An houre-glasse,
In which were sands but few,
    As he did passe,
He shew'd, and told me too,
    Mine end near was,
And so away he flew.

To his Peculiar Friend, M. Jo: Wicks.

Probably John Weekes, D.D , Prebend of Bristol, and Dean of St Burian in Cornwall ; a steadfast and congenial friend to Herrick, in good and evil fortune. Hesperides.

SINCE shed or cottage I have none,
I sing the more, that thou hast one ;
To whose glad threshold, and free door
I may a poet come, though poor ;
And eat with thee a savory bit,
Paying but common thanks for it.
Yet sho'd I chance, my Wicks, to see
An over-leven look in thee,
To soure the bread, and turn the beer
To an exalted vineger ;
Or sho'dst thou prize me as a dish
Of thrice-boyl'd-worts, or third dayes fish ;
I'de rather hungry go and come,
Then to thy house be burdensome ;
Yet, in my depth of grief, I'de be
One that sho'd drop his beads for thee.

—◊—

The Dirge of Jephthahs Daughter.

Sung by the Virgins.
Noble Numbers.

O THOU, the wonder of all dayes !
O paragon, and pearle of praise !
O Virgin-martyr, ever blest
          Above the rest
Of all the maiden-traine ! We come,
And bring fresh strewings to thy tombe.

Thus, thus, and thus we compasse round
Thy harmlesse and unhaunted ground ;
And as we sing thy dirge, we will
          The daffadill,
And other flowers, lay upon
(The altar of our love) thy stone.

Thou wonder of all maids, li'st here,
Of daughters all, the deerest deere ;
The eye of virgins ; nay, the queen
          Of this smooth green,
And all sweet meades ; from whence we get
The primrose, and the violet.

Too soon, too deere did Jephthah buy,
By thy sad losse, our liberty :
His was the bond and cov'nant, yet
          Thou paid'st the debt,
Lamented maid ! he won the day,
But for the conquest thou didst pay.

Lyric Poems.

Thy father brought with him along
The olive branch, and victors song :
He slew the Ammonites, we know,
       But to thy woe ;
And in the purchase of our peace,
The cure was worse than the disease.

For which obedient zeale of thine,
We offer here, before thy shrine,
Our sighs for storax, teares for wine ;
       And to make fine,
And fresh thy herse-cloth, we will, here,
Foure times bestrew thee ev'ry yeere.

Receive, for this thy praise, our teares :
Receive this offering of our haires :
Receive these christall vialls fil'd
       With teares, distil'd
From teeming eyes ; to these we bring,
Each maid, her silver filleting,

To guild thy tombe ; besides, these caules,
These laces, ribbands, and these faules,
These veiles, wherewith we used to hide
       The bashfull bride,
When we conduct her to her groome :
And, all we lay upon thy tombe.

No more, no more, since thou art dead,
Shall we ere bring coy brides to bed ;
No more, at yeerly festivalls
       We cowslip balls,
Or chaines of columbines shall make,
For this, or that occasions sake.

Herrick.

No, no ; our maiden-pleasures be
Wrapt in the winding-sheet, with thee :
'Tis we are dead, though not i'th'grave :
   Or, if we have
One seed of life left, 'tis to keep
A Lent for thee, to fast and weep.

Sleep in thy peace, thy bed of spice ;
And make this place all paradise :
May sweets grow here! and smoke from hence,
   Fat frankincense :
Let balme, and cassia send their scent
From out thy maiden-monument.

May no wolfe howle, or screech-owle stir
A wing about thy sepulcher !
No boysterous winds, or stormes, come hither,
   To starve, or wither
Thy soft sweet earth ! but, like a spring,
Love keep it ever flourishing.

May all shie maids, at wonted hours,
Come forth, to strew thy tombe with flow'rs :
May virgins, when they come to mourn,
   Male-incense burn
Upon thine altar ! then return,
And leave thee sleeping in thy urn.

—◦◦◦—

Comfort to a
Youth that had Hesperides.
lost his Love.

WHAT needs complaints,
When she a place
Has with the race
        Of saints ?
In endlesse mirth,
She thinks not on
What's said or done
        In earth :
She sees no teares,
Or any tone
Of thy deep grone
        She heares :
Nor do's she minde,
Or think on't now,
That ever thou
        Wast kind
But chang'd above,
She likes not there,
As she did here,
        Thy love.
Forbeare therefore,
And lull asleepe
Thy woes, and weep
        No more.

—ᴡᴡ—

Herrick.

The Christian Militant.

A MAN prepar'd against all ills to come,
    That dares to dead the fire of martirdome :
That sleeps at home ; and sayling there at ease,
Feares not the fierce sedition of the seas :
That's counter-proofe against the farms mis-
        haps,
Undreadfull too of courtly thunderclaps :
That weares one face, like heaven, and never
        showes
A change, when Fortune either comes, or goes :
That keepes his own strong guard, in the de-
        spight
Of what can hurt by day, or harme by night :
That takes and re-delivers every stroake
Of chance, as made up all of rock, and oake :
That sighs at other's death ; smiles at his own
Most dire and horrid crucifixion.
Who for true glory suffers thus ; we grant
Him to be here our Christian militant,

—◆—

173

To his Con-science.

Cᴀɴ I not sin, but thou wilt be
  My private protonotarie?
Can I not wooe thee to passe by
A short and sweet iniquity?
I'le cast a mist and cloud, upon
My delicate transgression,
So utter dark, as that no eye
Shall see the hug'd impietie :
Gifts blind the wise, and bribes do please,
And winde all other witnesses :
And wilt not thou, with gold, be ti'd
To lay thy pen and ink aside?
That in the mirk and tonguelesse night,
Wanton I may, and thou not write?
It will not be : and, therefore, now,
For times to come, I'le make this vow,
From aberrations to live free ;
So I'le not feare the Judge, or thee.

—⋙⋘—

Herrick.

To God. Noble Numbers.

Come to me God ; but do not come
To me, as to the gen'rall doome,
In power ; or come Thou in that state,
When Thou Thy lawes didst promulgate,
When as the mountains quak'd for dread,
And sullen clouds bound up his head.
No, lay thy stately terrours by,
To talke with me familiarly ;
For if Thy thunder-claps I heare,
I shall lesse swoone, then die for feare.
Speake thou of love and I'le reply
By way of epithalamie,
Or sing of mercy, and I'le suit
To it my violl and my lute :
Thus let Thy lips but love distill,
Then come my God, and hap what will.

—⁓⋀⋀⋎⋏⋎—

To God, on his Sicknesse. Noble Numbers.

What though my harp, and violl be
Both hung upon the willow-tree ?
What though my bed be now my grave,
And for my house I darknesse have ?
What though my healthfull dayes are fled
And I lie numbred with the dead ?
Yet I have hope, by Thy great power,
To spring ; though now a wither'd flower.

175

Lyric Poems.

To Anthea. Hesperides.

Sᴵᴄᴋ is Anthea, sickly is the spring,
The primrose sick, and sickly every thing :
The while my deer Anthea do's but droop,
The tulips, lillies, daffadills do stoop ;
But when again sh'as got her healthfull houre,
Each bending then, will rise a proper flower.

—ᴠᴠᴠᴠᴠ—

On Himselfe. Hesperides.

I.

Wᴇᴇᴘᴇ for the dead, for they have lost this
   light :
And weepe for me, lost in an endlesse night.
Or mourne, or make a marble verse for me,
Who writ for many. *Benedicite.*

II.

Lᴏsᴛ to the world ; lost to my selfe ; alone
Here now I rest under this marble stone :
In depth of silence, heard, and seene of none.

—ᴠᴠᴠᴠᴠ—

Buriall. Hesperides.

M<small>AN</small> may want land to live in; but for all,
Nature finds out some place for buriall.

—⟋⋁⋁⋁⋎—

The Apparition "Calling him to of his Mistresse: Elizium." Hesperides.

Desunt nonnulla——

C<small>OME</small> then, and like two doves with silv'rie
    wings,
Let our soules flie to'th'shades, where ever
    springs
Sit smiling in the meads; where balme and
    oile,
Roses and cassia crown the untill'd soyle.
Where no disease raignes, or infection comes
To blast the aire, but amber-greece and gums.
This, that, and ev'ry thicket doth transpire
More sweet, then storax from the hallowed
    fire :
Where ev'ry tree a wealthy issue beares
Of fragrant apples, blushing plums, or peares :
And all the shrubs, with sparkling spangels,
    shew
Like morning-sun-shine tinsilling the dew.
Here in green meddowes sits eternall May,
Purfling the margents, while perpetuall day

Lyric Poems.

So double gilds the aire, as that no night
Can ever rust th'enamel of the light.
Here, naked younglings handsome striplings
 run
Their goales for virgins kisses; which when
 done,
Then unto dancing forth the learned round
Commixt they meet, with endlesse roses crown'd.
And here we'l sit on primrose-banks, and see
Love's chorus led by Cupid ; and we'l be
Two loving followers too unto the grove,
Where poets sing the stories of our love.
There thou shalt hear divine Musæus sing
Of Hero, and Leander ; then Ile bring
Thee to the stand, where honour'd Homer
 reades
His Odisees, and his high Iliads.
About whose throne the crowd of poets throng
To heare the incantation of his tongue :
To Linus, then to Pindar ; and that done,
Ile bring thee Herrick to Anacreon,
Quaffing his full-crown'd bowles of burning
 wine,
And in his raptures speaking lines of thine,
Like to his subject ; and as his frantick-
Looks, shew him truly Bacchanalian like,
Besmear'd with grapes ; welcome he shall thee
 thither,
Where both may rage, both drink and dance
 together.
Then stately Virgil, witty Ovid, by
Whom faire Corinna sits, and doth comply
With yvorie wrists, his laureat head, and steeps
His eye in dew of kisses, while he sleeps.

Herrick.

Then soft Catullus, sharp-fang'd Martial,
And towring Lucan, Horace, Juvenal,
And snakie Perseus, these, and those, whom
    rage
(Dropt for the jarres of heaven) fill'd t'engage
All times unto their frenzies ; thou shalt there
Behold them in a spacious theater.
Among which glories, crown'd with sacred
    bayes,
And flatt'ring ivie, two recite their plaies,
Beumont and Fletcher, swans, to whom all
    eares
Listen, while they, like syrens in their spheres,
Sing their Evadne ; and still more for thee
There yet remaines to know, then thou can'st
    see
By glim'ring of a fancie : doe but come,
And there Ile shew thee that capacious roome
In which thy father Johnson now is plac't,
As in a globe of radiant fire, and grac't
To be in that orbe crown'd, that doth include
Those prophets of the former magnitude,
And he one chiefe ; but harke, I heare the
    cock,
The bell-man of the night, proclaime the clock
Of late struck one ; and now I see the prime
Of day break from the pregnant east, 'tis time
I vanish ; more I had to say ;
But night determines here, away.

—·/\/\/\~—

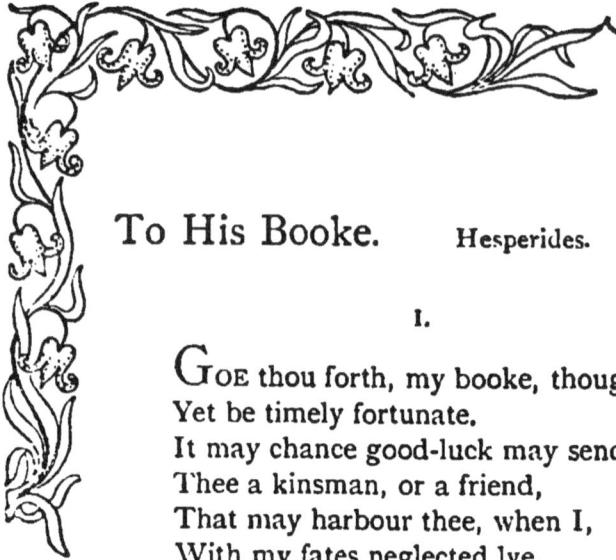

To His Booke. Hesperides.

I.

Goe thou forth, my booke, though late ;
Yet be timely fortunate.
It may chance good-luck may send
Thee a kinsman, or a friend,
That may harbour thee, when I,
With my fates neglected lye.
If thou know'st not where to dwell,
See, the fier's by : Farewell.

II.

Make haste away, and let one be
A friendly patron unto thee :
Lest rapt from hence, I see thee lye
Torn for the use of pasterie :
Or see thy injur'd leaves serve well,
To make loose gownes for mackarell :
Or see the grocers in a trice,
Make hoods of thee to serve out spice.

—\/\/\/—

Herrick.

Eternitie.

O YEARES ! and age ! farewell :
　　Behold I go,
　　Where I do know
Infinitie to dwell.

And these mine eyes shall see
　　All times, how they
　　Are lost i'th' sea
Of vast eternitie.

Where never moone shall sway
　　The starres ; but she,
　　And night, shall be
Drown'd in one endlesse day.

—ᗯᐯᐯᐯ—

The Last Line.

To his Book's end this last line he'd have
　　plac't,
Jocond his Muse was ; but his Life was chast.

PRINTED BY
TURNBULL AND SPEARS
EDINBURGH

www.ingramcontent.com/pod-product-compliance
Lightning Source LLC
Chambersburg PA
CBHW030830270326

41928CB00007B/985